AF483585

Table Of Contents

NOW I AM RICH. I was Rich before I was born, and when I was born, I forgot. Now I AM richer than ever because everything belongs to "ME", a unique, beloved Child. No Competition but the Power of Abundance.

To Correct In The Through Of Eternity

Now I Am Rich

Chapter 1: Before I Was Born

I was rich before I was born. Not in the sense of monetary wealth, but in the purest form of abundance that the universe can offer. It was a richness that transcended physical assets; itwas embedded in the very essence of my being. I was part of the universal energy, connected to everything and everyone. There was no sense of lack or need, only a profound understanding that everything I could ever desire was already mine.

Chapter 2: The Forgetting

When I was born, I forgot. The moment I entered the world, the richness that had been mybirthright was obscured by the limitations of the human experience. I was born into a family of modest means, and the society I entered placed immense value on material wealth. The richness of my true nature was overshadowed by the pursuit of money, possessions, and status.

Chapter 3: Childhood Innocence

As a child, I was blissfully unaware of the societal constructs that defined wealth. I found joy in the simplest of things—playing in the mud, chasing butterflies, and listening to the storiesmy parents told. In those moments, I was rich beyond measure, though I did not yet realize it. The world was a playground of endless possibilities, and my imagination was the only currency I needed.

Chapter 4: The First Glimpse of Lack

It wasn't long before I became aware of the concept of lack. I saw other children with toys I didn't have, wearing clothes I couldn't afford. I overheard conversations about bills, debts, and the constant struggle to make ends meet. Slowly, the seeds of scarcity were planted in my mind. I began to believe that to be truly happy, I needed more— more toys, more clothes, more money.

Chapter 5: The Pursuit Begins

As I grew older, my desire for material wealth intensified. I worked hard in school, driven bythe belief that academic success was the key to financial security. I pursued higher education, took on multiple jobs, and sacrificed sleep and social life in the quest for a better future. I was determined to escape the clutches of scarcity and claim my place among the wealthy.

Chapter 6: Early Success

My hard work paid off. I graduated with honors, landed a high-paying job, and started climbing the corporate ladder. With each promotion and pay raise, I felt a sense of accomplishment. I bought a beautiful house, a luxury car, and filled my life with the trappings of success. To the outside world, I was the epitome of wealth and prosperity.

Chapter 7: The Hollow Victory

Yet, despite my outward success, something was missing. I had all the money I could want, but the sense of abundance I had known before my birth eluded me. I was constantly stressed, always chasing the next goal, the next milestone. My relationships suffered, and the joy I had once found in simple pleasures was replaced by a relentless drive for more.

Chapter 8: The Turning Point

The turning point came unexpectedly. A health scare forced me to reevaluate my priorities. Lying in a hospital bed, I realized that all the money in the world couldn't buy me peace of mind or true happiness. I began to question the very foundation of my beliefs about wealthand success. Was it possible that the richness I sought was not something to be acquired,but something to be remembered?

Chapter 9: The Journey Within

I embarked on a journey within, seeking to reconnect with the abundance that was my birthright. I meditated, practiced mindfulness, and immersed myself in spiritual teachings. Slowly, I began to peel away the layers of societal conditioning that had clouded my perception. I remembered the richness that had always been mine, the inherent worth that had nothing to do with money or possessions.

Chapter 10: Reclaiming Abundance

With this newfound awareness, I began to live differently. I focused on gratitude, appreciating the abundance in every moment. I invested time in relationships, experiences, and personal growth rather than accumulating more stuff. I found joy in giving, sharing my wealth with others and making a positive impact on the world.

Chapter 11: The Power of Abundance

I realized that true abundance comes from within. It is the recognition that everything I need is already available to me, that I am connected to a limitless source of prosperity. There is no competition, no need to hoard or fear scarcity. The power of abundance lies in the understanding that the more I give, the more I receive.

Chapter 12: Living Richer Than Ever

Now, I am richer than ever. Not because of the money in my bank account or the assets I own, but because I live in a state of perpetual abundance. I wake up each day with a heart full of gratitude, knowing that I am supported by the universe. I have everything I need and more, and I share this wealth freely with those around me.

Chapter 13: A Legacy of Abundance

I am committed to leaving a legacy of abundance. I teach my

children that their worth is not determined by their possessions, but by the love and kindness they share with the world. I support causes that promote equality, sustainability, and the well-being of all. My wealth is not just for me; it is a tool to create a better world for future generations.

Chapter 14: The Abundance Mindset

An abundance mindset is a powerful thing. It shifts the focus from what is lacking to what is already present. It transforms challenges into opportunities and opens doors that were previously unseen. With an abundance mindset, I approach life with confidence, creativity, and a sense of endless possibilities.

Chapter 15: The Joy of Giving

One of the greatest joys of being rich is the ability to give. I support charities, help friends in need, and invest in my community. The act of giving enriches my life in ways that money alone never could. It deepens my connections with others and reinforces the truth that we are all part of a greater whole.

Chapter 16: Financial Freedom

Financial freedom is more than having enough money to pay the bills. It is the freedom to live life on my own terms, to pursue my passions, and to make choices that align with my values. With financial freedom, I can focus on what truly matters, without being constrained by financial worries.

Chapter 17: The Wealth of Health

Health is a vital component of true wealth. I prioritize my physical, mental, and emotional well-being, recognizing that without health, all the money in the world is meaningless. I invest in nutritious food, regular exercise, and practices that nurture my mind and spirit.

Chapter 18: Relationships and Riches

Relationships are the true riches of life. My connections with family, friends, and loved ones bring me joy, support, and a sense of belonging. I cherish these relationships and invest time and energy in nurturing them. They are the foundation of my happiness and the ultimate measure of my success.

Chapter 19: The Joy of Simplicity

Simplicity is a path to richness. By decluttering my life and focusing on what truly matters, Icreate space for joy and fulfillment. I find pleasure in simple things—a walk in nature, a heartfelt conversation, a moment of quiet reflection. These simple joys are the essence of a rich life.

Chapter 20: Purpose and Prosperity

Purpose is the driving force behind true prosperity. When I align my actions with my values and passions, I experience a deep sense of fulfillment. My work becomes a source of joy and contribution, rather than just a means to an end. Purpose transforms wealth into a meaningful, impactful force.

Chapter 21: The Abundance of Time

Time is one of the most valuable resources we have. I use my time wisely, prioritizing activities that bring me joy, growth, and connection. I avoid the trap of busyness for the sake of busyness and focus on being present in each moment. Time spent in alignment with my values is time well spent.

Chapter 22: The Power of Gratitude

Gratitude is a powerful practice that enhances my sense of abundance. By regularly acknowledging and appreciating the blessings in my life, I cultivate a mindset of abundance.Gratitude shifts my focus from what is missing to what is already present, enriching my life in countless ways.

Chapter 23: Abundance in Adversity

Even in times of adversity, I find abundance. Challenges and setbacks are opportunities forgrowth and learning. They remind me of the resilience and resourcefulness within me. By embracing adversity with an abundance mindset, I transform obstacles into stepping stones toward greater prosperity.

Chapter 24: The Wealth of Knowledge

Knowledge is a form of wealth that no one can take away. I am committed to lifelong learning, constantly seeking to expand my understanding and skills. This wealth of knowledge enriches my life, enhances my contributions to the world, and opens up new opportunities for growth and success.

Chapter 25: The Art of Receiving

Receiving is as important as giving in the flow of abundance. I am open to receiving love, support, opportunities, and wealth from others. By allowing myself to receive, I honor theinterconnectedness of all life and participate fully in the cycle of abundance.

Chapter 26: The Spiritual Wealth

Spiritual wealth is the foundation of true abundance. It is the recognition of my connection to a higher power and the infinite source of prosperity. My spiritual practices ground me in this truth and guide me in living a life of purpose, joy, and abundance.

Chapter 27: The Abundance of Nature

Nature is a constant reminder of the abundance that surrounds us. Everywhere I look, I see evidence of the Earth's infinite generosity. The lush forests, winding rivers, majestic mountains, and vast oceans testify to this abundance. Every leaf, every drop of water, and every grain of sand is a part of this immeasurable wealth.

I find peace and inspiration in the beauty of the natural world. Nature, with its symphony of colors, sounds, and textures, is an inexhaustible source of serenity and creativity. When I walk through the forest, the scent of pine, the song of birds, and the rustle of leaves under my feet soothe my spirit. It is in these moments of deep connection with the earth that I feel most alive and in harmony with myself.

A swim in the ocean reminds me of the power and vastness of life. The waves crashing on the shore carry with them the energy of the entire world. Swimming in these invigorating waters, feeling the salty caress of the waves on my skin, immerses me in a state of gratitude and reverence. Every movement in the water is a dance with the vastness, a reminder that I am part of something greater.

Sitting in my garden is an act of contemplation and gratitude. The garden is a microcosm of nature, a space where life flourishes in miniature. The vibrant flowers, fragrant herbs, and fruit trees are daily gifts that nourish my soul. Observing the growth cycle of plants, I gained a deeper understanding of the natural rhythm of life and the patience it requires. Every blooming flower, every ripening fruit, is a silent celebration of abundance.

Nature nourishes my spirit in multiple ways. It teaches me resilience through trees that withstand storms, the perseverance of rivers carving valleys, and the generosity of plants offering their fruits without expectation. It inspires me to live fully, embrace each moment with gratitude, and recognize beauty in the simplest details.

In short, nature is a wise and generous teacher. It teaches me the importance of balance, patience, and gratitude. Through it, I discover every day the abundance that surrounds me and resides within me. By connecting with nature, I connect with my own essence, the inexhaustible source of peace, joy, and creativity that lies at the heart of the universe.

The Power of the Decision to BE Rich

Being is my identity, what I am: The Great "I AM." I have chosen to be what I decide to be, for "As He is, so are we." It is imperative to remember that "as a man thinketh in his heart, so is he."

Now I AM Free and Rich because I AM the Expression of Freedom.

The power of decision lies in our ability to choose our identity. When we decide to BE rich, we adopt a mindset of abundance and prosperity. This conscious choice transforms our reality, for our thoughts and beliefs shape our existence.

Being rich is not just about material possessions but an affirmation of our intrinsic worth and unlimited potential. By declaring, "I AM Free and Rich," we affirm our power to create our destiny and attract the opportunities and resources necessary for our fulfillment.

Let us always remember that our state of BEING reflects our deepest thoughts. By cultivating a positive and assertive vision of ourselves, we align our lives with the principles of success and freedom. Thus, every day, we embody the greatness of the "Great I AM" and live our full potential as free and rich beings.

It is imperative to decide with certainty when it comes to embracing one's personal identity. This is to live a life of abundance and freedom.

Our power of eternity is our primary energy, allowing us to manifest the wealth, abundance, and freedom for which we are destined and created—it is our merit.

The Power of Words and Decrees

Words are a powerful tool, a vector of creation and transformation. By the power of words, our decrees transcend the material world and automatically create what is decreed. For words are the very fabric of creation, and it is said that "whatever you say shall come to pass," for the Word is God.

When we speak words with conviction and intention, we activate a divine force capable of reshaping our reality. Every word we utter carries within it the potential to manifest profound and lasting changes. Our words, like seeds, germinate and grow, shaping the universe around us.

The power of words lies in their ability to materialize our thoughts and desires. By formulating decrees, we affirm our will and faith in their realization. This affirmation triggers a series of vibrations and energies that work towards the materialization of our wishes. Thus, by saying "I am rich" or "I am free," we are not merely making a declaration but breathing life into these potential realities.

The Word, as God's manifestation, holds unlimited creative power. It is the very essence of existence, the foundation of all that is. By aligning ourselves with this truth, we become co-creators, capable of transforming our lives and our environment simply by speaking with intention and faith.

It is crucial to recognize that every word we speak is an act of creation. By cultivating a keen awareness of this truth, we can direct our words toward positivity and elevation. By deliberately choosing words of love, prosperity, and freedom, we plant the seeds of a bright and abundant future.

In conclusion, words are a divine force, a sacred tool of creation. Through our decrees, we have the power to transcend the limits of the material world and manifest our deepest desires. Let us remember that "whatever you say shall come to pass," for the Word is God, and in it lies the infinite power to create, transform, and elevate.

Decrees

Just as a silent prayer or meditation, everything we focus on will manifest sooner or later because even thoughts are the first silent words. This is why this thought remains active: "As a man thinketh in his heart, so is he," and "whatever you say shall come to pass."

Decrees of Wealth

- I am rich.

- I am immensely rich.

- I am rich and in good health.

- I am immensely rich and happy.

- I am rich beyond measure.

- I am a source of infinite abundance.

- I am prosperous and thriving in all aspects of my life.

- I am financially free and secure.

- I am a magnet for wealth and opportunities.

- I am surrounded by prosperity and success.

- I am rich and generous.

- I am capable of creating and multiplying wealth.

- I am rich and deeply grateful for all that I have.

- I am a person of value and deserve great abundance.

- I am at peace with the wealth I attract.

- I am a living manifestation of divine prosperity.

- I am rich, and my success inspires others.

- I am a creator of wealth for myself and those around me.

- I am rich and filled with opportunities.

- I am immensely rich and blessed.

- I am Rich and Glorious.

- I am Rich now and forevermore.

By affirming these decrees daily, we invoke the power of words to attract and manifest wealth in our lives.

I Am the Expression of Freedom

I am the expression of freedom. This statement is not merely an assertion but a declaration of my true being and deep nature. Freedom is not an external condition but an intrinsic quality that resides within me at every moment and in every aspect of my life.

Freedom, for me, is primarily the freedom to be. It is the ability to express myself fully without constraint or fear of judgment. It is the possibility to follow my unique path, to listen to my inner voice, guided by the Thought of Eternity, and to live in accordance with my values and desires. By affirming my freedom to be, I claim my right to authenticity and personal fulfillment.

I am free in my thoughts and beliefs. I recognize that my thoughts create my reality, and I choose to nurture thoughts that are appropriate, rich, constructive, and elevated. I am aware that each thought is a seed that germinates and grows, shaping my life and environment. By cultivating thoughts of freedom, peace, and prosperity, I create a world where these qualities can flourish.

Freedom Requires Action

My freedom is also the freedom to act. I am the master and authority over my choices and actions. Every decision I make is an act of creation, a manifestation of my personal power. I am responsible for my life, and I choose to direct it toward well-being, growth, and abundance. By acting with intention and determination, I bring my aspirations to life and realize my potential.

I am the expression of wealth. My true wealth is not measured solely by material possessions but also by health, relationships, knowledge, and experiences. I am rich in talents and skills, love and compassion, curiosity and wisdom. Every aspect of my life is a source of wealth, and I recognize and celebrate this abundance every day.

Like freedom, wealth is a state of mind. By perceiving myself as rich, I attract abundance into my life. I am open to opportunities, and I know that the universe supports me in all my endeavors.

The Power of Freedom

My freedom is an inner force that transcends external circumstances. It is the power to choose, create, and manifest my reality according to my will and intention. Freedom means that I am not bound by expectations or limitations imposed by others or by myself. It is the recognition that I am the master of my destiny, capable of shaping my life in alignment with my deepest values and aspirations.

Freedom manifests in my ability to think freely, act with integrity, and follow the path that resonates with my heart. It allows me to live authentically and express my truths without fear of judgment or rejection. Every decision I make is an affirmation of my sovereignty, a conscious act of creation that reflects my unique identity.

My Nature of Wealth

My wealth is intrinsically linked to my true nature. It goes beyond material possessions to encompass abundance in all its forms: love, joy, health, knowledge, and creativity. Wealth is an expression of the infinite abundance of the universe, which manifests through me and in my daily life.

By recognizing my rich nature, I connect with the inexhaustible source of prosperity that resides within me. I am capable of creating and attracting opportunities, resources, and experiences that enrich my life and the lives of others. My wealth is a reflection of my intrinsic value, of my ability to give and receive, to share and multiply blessings.

My True Self

My true self is a divine expression of freedom and wealth. By connecting with this essence, I discover inner peace, deep joy, and contentment. I realize that everything I need to live a full and abundant life is already within me. Recognizing this truth opens me up to a life of fullness, where every moment is an opportunity for growth, gratitude, and celebration.

I am the expression of freedom, a creative force capable of transforming my reality. My nature of wealth is the embodiment of divine abundance, an inexhaustible source of prosperity and joy. By living in harmony with my true self, I manifest a life of freedom, wealth, and happiness, inspiring those around me to discover their own unlimited potential.

In conclusion, being the expression of freedom means living in alignment with my authentic and rich nature. It is a journey of self-discovery where every step is an affirmation of my inner power and divine potential. By embracing this truth, I create a life filled with abundance, freedom, and happiness, reflecting the greatness of the universe in every aspect of my existence.

My Power of Choice and Decision is Non-Negotiable

My power of choice and decision is non-negotiable. These fundamental attributes define my freedom and autonomy. By recognizing and affirming this truth, I become aware of my ability to shape my life on my own terms, without compromise or concession.

The Power of Choice

The power of choice is the very essence of freedom. Every moment of my life offers me a multitude of options and paths to follow. By exercising my power of choice, I take responsibility for my life and commit to living authentically, in alignment with my values and aspirations. My choice is not influenced by fear or external expectations but guided by my inner wisdom and personal vision.

Making conscious choices allows me to create a reality that reflects my deepest desires and cherished dreams. Whether in small daily decisions or major life directions, every choice I make is an affirmation of my freedom and sovereignty.

The Power of Decision

The power of decision is the force that transforms my choices into concrete actions. To decide is to act with determination and clarity, to move forward with confidence on the path I have drawn. My decisions are made with a deep understanding of their impacts and implications, and I fully assume them.

By exercising my power of decision, I take control of my destiny and free myself from doubts and hesitations. Every decision is a step towards the realization of my goals and the manifestation of my dreams. My power of decision gives me the strength to overcome obstacles and transform challenges into opportunities.

The Intransigence of My Power

My power of choice and decision is non-negotiable. It cannot be compromised or delegated. They are the pillars of my integrity and personal freedom. By affirming this intransigence, I protect myself from negative influences and external pressures that could seek to limit my ability to live fully and freely.

My commitment to my power of choice and decision is a declaration of my worth and my inalienable right to self-determination. I am the creator of my life, and every choice and decision I make is an expression of my identity and unique vision.

In conclusion, recognizing that my power of choice and decision is non-negotiable is to affirm my sovereignty and personal freedom. It is to live with the conviction that I am the master of my destiny, capable of creating a life rich in meaning, abundance, and satisfaction. By honoring this power, I manifest a life aligned with my deepest values and highest aspirations, reflecting the greatness and freedom of my true self.

The Tranquility of Mind and Listening to One's Heart

The tranquility of mind requires listening to one's heart to receive the guidance and direction that reveals itself to us. By cultivating this attentive and sincere listening, we open ourselves to a deep source of inner wisdom that guides us with clarity and kindness through the complexities of life.

Listening to One's Heart

Listening to one's heart is about tuning in to one's feelings, intuitions, and deep aspirations. It is about taking the time to reconnect with oneself, away from the noise and distractions of the outside world. This inner listening is essential to achieving peace of mind because it puts us in touch with our true essence and desires.

The Path of the Heart

When we listen to our heart, we receive subtle but powerful messages that show us the way forward. This inner guidance is often felt as an intuition or deep conviction. It can manifest as feelings of peace, certainty, or excitement at the prospect of taking a particular direction. By following this guidance, we align our actions with our inner truth, leading to a more harmonious and fulfilling life.

The Revelation of Direction

Peace of mind is not only found in silence but in action illuminated by the wisdom of the heart. By listening to our heart, we allow our mind to calm and clear. This mental clarity helps us discern the choices and decisions that align with our well-being and fulfillment. Directions naturally reveal themselves when we are in harmony with our heart, as we become receptive to the signs and synchronicities that mark our path.

Peace and Listening to the Heart

Peace of mind is inseparable from inner peace. This peace is the result of listening to our heart and trusting its guidance. By following the path of our hearts, we find a sense of security and serenity, even in the face of life's challenges and uncertainties. We know that we are on the right path, the one destined for us, and this brings us lasting and profound peace.

In Brief

Peace of mind requires listening to one's heart. By cultivating this listening, we open ourselves to inner guidance that illuminates our path and leads us toward a more authentic and fulfilling life. Listening to our hearts means honoring our true essence, following our intuition, and acting in alignment with our deepest aspirations. It is in this inner harmony that we find true peace of mind, a peace that transcends external circumstances and allows us to navigate life with confidence and serenity.

Wealth and Wisdom

What is Wealth without Wisdom?

"The fear of the Lord is the beginning of wisdom, and the knowledge of the holy is understanding. For by me thy days shall be multiplied, and the years of thy life shall be increased. If thou be wise, thou shalt be wise for thyself: but if thou scornest, thou alone shalt bear it."

Proverbs 9:10-12 (Revised)

Wisdom is worth far more than gold and diamonds. While material wealth can be gained and lost, wisdom stays with us, guiding our decisions and enriching our lives in a profound and lasting way. To be wise is to possess a deep understanding of life, an ability to discern the right path, and a serenity in the face of challenges. By cultivating wisdom, you accumulate invaluable wealth that cannot be measured in financial terms. Therefore, by developing your wisdom, you are truly rich, for this inner wealth transcends material possessions and brings genuine and lasting fulfillment.

Revised Version:

Wisdom is worth far more than gold and diamonds. While material wealth can be gained and lost, wisdom stays with us, illuminating our choices and enriching our lives in a deep and lasting way. To possess wisdom is to have a deep understanding of life, to know how to discern the right path, and to remain serene in the face of challenges. By cultivating wisdom, you accumulate invaluable wealth far beyond any financial measure. Thus, by nurturing your wisdom, you become truly rich, for this inner wealth transcends material possessions and brings authentic and eternal fulfillment.

Bible Verses

Matthew 12:42 (KJV):

"The queen of the south shall rise up in the judgment with this generation, and shall condemn it: for she came from the uttermost parts of the earth to hear the wisdom of Solomon; and, behold, a greater than Solomon is here."

Revelation 5:12 (KJV):

"Saying with a loud voice, Worthy is the Lamb that was slain to receive power, and riches, and wisdom, and strength, and honour, and glory, and blessing."

Ecclesiastes 2:13 (KJV):

"Then I saw that wisdom excelleth folly, as far as light excelleth darkness."

1 Corinthians 1:21 (KJV):

"For after that in the wisdom of God the world by wisdom knew not God, it pleased God by the foolishness of preaching to save them that believe."

Jeremiah 10:12 (KJV):

"He hath made the earth by his power, he hath established the world by his wisdom, and hath stretched out the heavens by his discretion."

Jeremiah 51:15 (KJV):

"He hath made the earth by his power, he hath established the world by his wisdom, and hath stretched out the heaven by his understanding."

Daniel 2:20 (KJV):

"Daniel answered and said, Blessed be the name of God for ever and ever: for wisdom and might are his."

2 Peter 3:15 (KJV):

"And account that the longsuffering of our Lord is salvation; even as our beloved brother Paul also according to the wisdom given unto him hath written unto you."

Job 12:13 (KJV):

"With him is wisdom and strength, he hath counsel and understanding."

James 3:13 (KJV):

"Who is a wise man and endued with knowledge among you? let him shew out of a good conversation his works with meekness of wisdom."

1 Corinthians 2:7 (KJV):

"But we speak the wisdom of God in a mystery, even the hidden wisdom, which God ordained before the world unto our glory."

Ecclesiastes 7:12 (KJV):

"For wisdom is a defence, and money is a defence: but the excellency of knowledge is, that wisdom giveth life to them that have it."

2 Corinthians 4:6 (KJV):

"For God, who commanded the light to shine out of darkness, hath shined in our hearts, to give the light of the knowledge of the glory of God in the face of Jesus Christ."

Revelation 5:13 (KJV):

"And every creature which is in heaven, and on the earth, and under the earth, and such as are in the sea, and all that are in them, heard I saying, Blessing, and honour, and glory, and power, be unto him that sitteth upon the throne, and unto the Lamb for ever and ever."

Romans 11:33 (KJV):

"O the depth of the riches both of the wisdom and knowledge of God! how unsearchable are his judgments, and his ways past finding out!"

Isaiah 45:18 (KJV):

"For thus saith the Lord that created the heavens; God himself that formed the earth and made it; he hath established it, he created it not in vain, he formed it to be inhabited: I am the Lord; and there is none else."

Psalm 104:24 (KJV):

"O Lord, how manifold are thy works! in wisdom hast thou made them all: the earth is full of thy riches."

Ephesians 3:9 (KJV):

"And to make all men see what is the fellowship of the mystery, which from the beginning of the world hath been hid in God, who created all things by Jesus Christ:"

Genesis 1:1 (KJV):

"In the beginning God created the heaven and the earth."

Revelation 1:6 (KJV):

"And hath made us kings and priests unto God and his Father; to him be glory and dominion for ever and ever. Amen."

Zechariah 12:1 (KJV):

"The burden of the word of the Lord for Israel, saith the Lord, which stretcheth forth the heavens, and layeth the foundation of the earth, and formeth the spirit of man within him."

Isaiah 42:5 (KJV):

"Thus saith God the Lord, he that created the heavens, and stretched them out; he that spread forth the earth, and that which cometh out of it; he that giveth breath unto the people upon it, and spirit to them that walk therein:"

Romans 1:20 (KJV):

"For the invisible things of him from the creation of the world are clearly seen, being understood by the things that are made, even his eternal power and Godhead; so that they are without excuse:"

2 Corinthians 5:17 (KJV):

"Therefore if any man be in Christ, he is a new creature: old things are passed away; behold, all things are become new."

Titus 2:11 (KJV):

"For the grace of God that bringeth salvation hath appeared to all men,"

Revelation 5:12 (KJV):

"Saying with a loud voice, Worthy is the Lamb that was slain to receive power, and riches, and wisdom, and strength, and honour, and glory, and blessing."

Silence and Concentration

To live freely and richly, it is essential to savor moments of silence and listen to your heart. In a world that is constantly noisy and agitated, finding moments of tranquility allows you to reconnect with yourself. By listening to your heart, you discover your true desires and aspirations, leading to a more fulfilled and authentic life. Richness is not measured solely in financial terms but also in inner peace and personal satisfaction. Appreciating these moments of silence and introspection is the key to achieving true freedom and deep wealth.

The Word is Yours and Within You

The Word is Power and Fortune.

"Death and life are in the power of the tongue: and they that love it shall eat the fruit thereof." (Proverbs 18:21, KJV)

Whoever loves the Word will inevitably enjoy its fruits.

The coaching industry, mentorship, preaching, conferences, consulting, journalism, media, oratory art, and negotiation are all founded on the Word. The Word is the fabric of creation, from which all creation emerges.

Through the Word, you can sell illusion and fiction, which the wise can transform into reality because all things are possible to those who possess the Power of Conviction associated with the Word. If you have the Word, you have Fortune. However, this requires firmness and persistence.

The importance of the Word cannot be overstated. It is the tool with which we shape our reality, influence others, and connect on a deep level. The Word is more than just a means of communication; it is a creative force. By mastering it, you become the master of your destiny.

The Power of the Word

1. **Creation and Manifestation**

   The Word is the primary tool of creation. Everything that exists has been named and thus came into existence through the Word. Great works, successful enterprises, cultural revolutions, and social movements all begin with words.

2. **Influence and Leadership**

   Leaders use the Word to inspire, motivate, and guide. Famous speeches that changed the course of history are examples of the power of the Word in action. The ability to persuade and influence through words is an invaluable skill in all areas of life.

3. **Personal Transformation**

   The Word has the power to transform your life. Through positive affirmations and constructive self-talk, you can reprogram your mind and change limiting beliefs. The Word can heal, inspire, and elevate.

4. **Relationships and Communication**

   The quality of your relationships is directly proportional to the quality of your communication. A well-chosen word can strengthen bonds, resolve conflicts, and create deep connections.

Mastering the Word

1. **Clarity and Precision**

    For the Word to be powerful, it must be clear and precise.
    Avoid ambiguities and generalities. Be specific in what you
    express.

2. **Authenticity**

    Speak with sincerity and integrity. Words that come from
    the heart resonate more deeply and have a lasting impact.

3. **Positivity**

    Use the Word to build, not destroy. Positive and
    encouraging words not only uplift others but also attract
    positive energy into your life.

4. **Conviction**

    Believe in what you say. Conviction gives power to your
    words and inspires confidence and certainty in those who
    listen to you.

The Word is a divine gift, a powerful force that resides within each
of us. By becoming aware of its power and using it with wisdom and
discernment, we can transform our reality, achieve our goals, and create
a life rich in meaning and success. Let your Words be a reflection of
your inner greatness and a tool for creating your most noble
aspirations.

The Power of Coherence and Alignment: Keys to Abundance

Abundance in life does not simply result from luck or chance. It is the fruit of a conscious process of coherence and alignment. When our thoughts, words, and actions are in harmony, we create a state of coherence that naturally attracts abundance.

Coherence: Foundation of Abundance

Coherence is the congruence between our inner beliefs and our outer actions. It implies deep integrity where every aspect of our being is in agreement with our values and aspirations. This coherence creates a magnetic force that attracts the opportunities and resources needed to achieve our goals.

1. **Thoughts and Beliefs**

   o Our thoughts and beliefs form the basis of our reality. When we cultivate positive thoughts aligned with our goals, we create coherent energy that attracts abundance.

   o Limiting beliefs must be replaced with beliefs that support our vision of abundance. For example, believing in our own worth and ability to succeed is essential for manifesting abundance.

2. **Words and Affirmations**

   o The words we use are powerful. They can either reinforce our state of coherence or disrupt it. Using positive affirmations aligned with our desires strengthens our inner state and attracts abundance.

o   Speaking with intention and sincerity creates a harmonious vibration that resonates with the universe, thus facilitating the attraction of what we desire.

3. **Actions and Behaviors**

o   Our actions must reflect our thoughts and words. When we act in coherence with our beliefs and affirmations, we materialize our intentions and create a reality of abundance.

o   Every action taken should be aligned with our vision and goals, thereby reinforcing our path to abundance.

Alignment: Creating a Flow of Abundance

Alignment is the harmonization of our energy with the universal forces of abundance. It is a state where we resonate with the positive vibrations of the universe, thus facilitating the flow of abundance into our lives.

4. **Clear Vision and Intention**

o   Having a clear vision of what we want to attract into our lives is crucial. Alignment begins by defining our goals and desires with precision.

o   A clear and focused intention acts like a magnet, attracting circumstances and opportunities that resonate with our vision.

5. **Inner Listening and Intuition**

o   Alignment with abundance involves listening to our inner voice and following our intuition. These inner guides direct us towards actions and decisions that promote abundance.

o   Trusting our intuition and acting accordingly places us in a state of flow where synchronicities and miracles can occur.

6. **Gratitude and Positivity**

o   Cultivating an attitude of gratitude and positivity is essential for maintaining a state of alignment. Gratitude amplifies our positive vibration and attracts even more abundance.

o   By acknowledging and appreciating current blessings, we open the door to new opportunities for abundance.

The power of coherence and alignment is immense. By harmonizing our thoughts, words, and actions, and aligning ourselves with universal forces, we create a magnetic state that attracts abundance into our lives. This conscious and intentional approach not only transforms our external reality but also our inner state, allowing us to live a rich and fulfilling life. Abundance is not an accident; it is the result of carefully cultivated coherence and alignment. By adopting this perspective, we become the architects of our own abundance.

Who Doesn't Want to Be Rich?

In any case, it is in your nature to be rich—period.

In our modern society, wealth is often seen as the pinnacle of success and personal fulfillment. But beyond the stereotypes and clichés, it's worth asking: who doesn't want to be rich?

The Universal Appeal of Wealth

Most people aspire to wealth, and for good reasons. Wealth provides opportunities, freedoms, and securities that many seek to achieve:

1. **Financial Security**

   o Wealth provides peace of mind by eliminating financial worries. It covers essential needs such as housing, food, and medical care without stress.

   o Having financial reserves allows you to handle unexpected events and emergencies, offering reassuring stability.

2. **Opportunities and Freedom**

   o Being rich offers the freedom to choose your lifestyle, hobbies, and passions without being limited by financial constraints.

   o Wealth enables investment in education, travel, and enriching experiences that broaden your horizons and understanding of the world.

3. **Impact and Contribution**

o With financial resources, it is possible to support important causes, contribute to charities, and make a positive impact on society.

o Wealth also allows you to create jobs, launch innovative projects, and support community initiatives.

The Flip Side

However, not everyone pursues wealth in the same way, and some even choose to turn away from it. Why?

1. **Values and Priorities**

o Some people prioritize values such as simplicity, authenticity, and living in harmony with nature, which are often perceived as incompatible with the relentless pursuit of wealth.

o For some, material wealth does not bring the same level of satisfaction as personal relationships, spiritual growth, or the pursuit of creative passions.

2. **Stress and Pressure**

o The pursuit of wealth can often come with immense stress and constant pressure to succeed, sometimes at the expense of mental and physical health.

o Managing large amounts of money and the responsibilities that come with it can also be a source of tension and conflict.

3. **Satisfaction and Contentment**

o Some people find deep contentment in a simple and minimalist life. They believe that happiness does not lie in accumulating wealth but in appreciating the small things in life.

o The philosophy of "less is more" is gaining popularity, encouraging a streamlined and intentional life.

So, who doesn't want to be rich? The answer is complex and nuanced. While wealth offers many opportunities and benefits, it is not a universal aspiration. Personal values, life priorities, and sources of satisfaction vary greatly from person to person. In the end, true wealth may reside in each individual's ability to define what brings happiness and meaning to their own life, whether that is material wealth or other forms of spiritual and emotional richness.

Financial Education: A Simple and Engaging Strategy for the Wealth Adventure

Financial education is the key to unlocking the doors to wealth and financial freedom. Understanding how to manage, invest, and grow your money is essential for anyone looking to improve their economic situation. Here's a simple and engaging strategy to embark on this exciting adventure.

Understanding the Basics

1. Budgeting and Expense Management

   o **Create a budget:** Record your income and expenses to get an overview of your financial situation. A well-planned budget helps you avoid overspending and save effectively.

   o **Reduce unnecessary expenses:** Identify and eliminate superfluous spending. Prioritize essential needs and set savings goals.

2. Savings and Emergency Funds

   o **Automatic savings:** Set up automatic transfers to a savings account. This allows you to save regularly without having to think about it.

o   **Emergency fund:** Build an emergency fund equivalent to three to six months of expenses to handle unexpected situations without resorting to debt.

Investing for the Future

1.   **Simple and Effective Investments**

o   **Investment accounts:** Open accounts such as a Stocks and Shares ISA or an Individual Retirement Account (IRA). They offer tax benefits that can maximize your returns.

o   **Diversification:** Invest in a diversified portfolio of stocks, bonds, and index funds to reduce risks.

2.   **Understanding Financial Markets**

o   **Ongoing education:** Read books, take online courses, and listen to podcasts on investing and personal finance. The more you know, the better equipped you'll be to make informed decisions.

o   **Monitor investments:** Regularly review your investments to ensure they align with your financial goals and adjust them as needed.

Managing Debt

1.   **Strategies for Eliminating Debt**

o   **Prioritize high-interest debt:** Focus first on paying off debts with the highest interest rates. This will allow you to reduce the total amount of interest paid more quickly.

o   **Debt consolidation:** If you have multiple debts, consider consolidating them into a single loan with a lower interest rate to simplify your payments and reduce costs.

2. **Avoid Excessive Borrowing**

o   **Use credit wisely:** Do not spend more than you can repay. Limit the use of credit cards and prefer cash or debit card payments.

o   **Avoid costly consumer loans:** Be cautious with high-interest loans, such as revolving credit. Prefer low-cost financing options.

Adopting a Wealth Mindset

1. Develop a Growth Mindset

o   **Set clear financial goals:** Define short-term, medium-term, and long-term goals. They will give you direction and motivation to achieve wealth.

o   **Be persistent and patient:** Wealth is not built overnight. Be patient, stay committed to your goals, and persevere despite obstacles.

2. **Ongoing Education and Adaptation**

o   **Stay informed:** The financial world is constantly evolving. Continue educating yourself and adapting your strategies based on new knowledge and economic changes.

o   **Learn from mistakes:** Don't be discouraged by financial errors. See them as learning opportunities and adjust your approaches to succeed better in the future.

Financial education is a fascinating and enriching journey. By adopting simple and well-thought-out strategies, you can not only improve your financial situation but also pave the way to wealth and freedom. Start today, stay informed, plan, and make informed decisions for a prosperous financial future.

Focusing on Abundance and Nothing Else

The key to attracting wealth and success in your life lies in your ability to focus exclusively on abundance and to remove anything that might distract you. Abundance is not only about material wealth but also includes health, relationships, and joy. Here's how focusing solely on abundance can transform your life.

1.   **Adopt an Abundance Mindset: Change Your Perspective**

o   **Think in terms of possibilities:** Embrace the idea that the world is full of endless opportunities. Every situation, even challenges, offers a chance for growth and success.

o   **Eliminate limiting beliefs:** Identify and remove beliefs that hold you back. Replace them with positive affirmations and visions of success.

2. **Gratitude and Recognition**

o **Practice daily gratitude:** Start each day by noting three things you are grateful for. This refocuses your mind on what you already have and opens the door to more abundance.

o **Recognize your achievements:** Celebrate even small victories. Each step forward is proof that abundance is already present in your life.

3. **Create an Abundant Environment: Surround Yourself with Positivity**

o **Choose your company wisely:** Spend time with people who share a growth and abundance mindset. Their positive energy will support you in your quest.

o **Consume inspiring media:** Read books, listen to podcasts, and watch videos that promote positive thinking and success.

4. **Organize Your Space**

o **Declutter:** A tidy physical space reflects a clear mind. Remove clutter to create an environment conducive to focus and productivity.

o **Add motivational elements:** Display inspiring quotes, visions of your goals, and symbols of success in your workspace and living area.

5. **Take Inspired Actions: Set Clear Goals**

o **Set SMART goals:** Specific, Measurable, Achievable, Realistic, and Time-bound goals give you clear direction and motivate you to act.

o **Visualize success:** Spend a few minutes each day visualizing your goals achieved. Feel the positive emotions associated with your success.

6. **Take Action**

o **Act daily:** Do at least one thing each day that brings you closer to your goals. Consistent actions lead to extraordinary results.

o **Learn and adapt:** Regularly evaluate your progress and adjust your strategies if necessary. Be flexible and open to new opportunities.

7. **Cultivate a Balanced Life: Physical and Mental Well-being**

o **Take care of your health:** A healthy diet, regular exercise, and sufficient sleep are essential for maintaining a clear mind and high energy levels.

o **Meditate and relax:** Meditation and relaxation techniques help reduce stress and maintain a positive mindset.

8. **Balance Work and Leisure**

   o **Prioritize quality time:** Spend time with loved ones, engage in activities that you are passionate about, and take regular breaks to recharge.

   o **Maintain hobbies:** Having enriching hobbies helps you stay creative and motivated, balancing the professional and personal aspects of your life.

Focusing on abundance and nothing else is a powerful approach to transforming your life. By adopting an abundance mindset, creating a positive environment, taking inspired actions, and cultivating a balanced life, you will naturally attract wealth and success into every aspect of your existence. Start today by directing your attention towards abundance, and watch how your world fills with endless possibilities.

Replacing the Idea of Lack with a Debt of Love

In a world often focused on materialism and competition, we tend to concentrate on what we lack. This mentality of scarcity can trap us in a vicious cycle of fear and dissatisfaction. What if we replaced this notion of lack with the idea of "debt of love"? Imagine filling your love bank account and constantly offering that love to the world through the power of your imagination. The impact is phenomenal, as we are never truly separated from one another.

1. **Transformation through Love: Change Your Perspective**

o **See abundance everywhere:** Instead of focusing on what you don't have, notice the love and generosity that exist around you. The world is filled with kindness and opportunities to give and receive love.

o **Reprogram your mind:** Replace thoughts of lack with affirmations of abundance. Tell yourself daily that love is infinite and surrounds you constantly.

2. **Cultivate Gratitude**

o **Practice gratitude for received love:** Every act of kindness, every smile, every moment of connection is proof of the abundance of love in your life. Be grateful for these moments.

o **Express your gratitude:** Share your appreciation with others. A simple "thank you" can strengthen bonds of love and generosity.

3. **Filling Your Love Bank Account: Imagine Love as Currency**

o **Visualize a love account:** Imagine that every act of love you give or receive fills an imaginary bank account. This account never diminishes; it only increases with each gesture of kindness and compassion.

o **Invest in love:** Like a wise investor, choose to "deposit" love each day. Send positive thoughts, perform acts of kindness, and show compassion.

4. **Constantly Offer Love**

o **Give without expecting a return:** True love expects nothing in return. Give freely and generously, knowing that each act of love enriches not only those who receive it but also yourself.

o **Use imagination to create love:** Let your imagination guide you in finding new and creative ways to show love. Write appreciation letters, create artwork, or simply offer your time and attention.

5. The Phenomenal Impact of Love: The Power of Connection

- o **Understand our interconnectedness:** We are never truly separate. Every person you touch with an act of love will touch others, creating an endless chain of positivity and connection.

- o **Strengthen human bonds:** Love creates strong, lasting connections. By constantly offering love, you contribute to a more united and harmonious world.

6. **Creating a World of Abundance**

- o **Multiply abundance:** Love given multiplies. Each act of love creates a ripple effect, increasing abundance for all. By filling the world with love, you transform the collective reality.

- o **Live in abundance:** By focusing on love rather than lack, you live in a state of abundance. This perspective transforms your life, bringing more joy, peace, and satisfaction.

Replacing the idea of lack with the debt of love is a radically transformative approach. By imagining that you are filling your love bank account and constantly offering that love to the world, you create a phenomenal impact. For in truth, we are never separate; we are all connected by the invisible threads of love. Adopt this mindset and see how the abundance of love enriches every aspect of your life and the lives of others.

Living a Life of Wealth: Personal Determination and Resilience

Living a truly wealthy life requires freeing ourselves from the idea that we must rely on others to accomplish what we are supposed to do ourselves. Collaboration is essential, certainly, but the foundation of our determination and resilience must be forged within ourselves, through continuous and dedicated effort.

1. **Independence as the Foundation of Wealth: Autonomy and Responsibility**

- o **Take charge of your destiny:** True wealth begins with taking responsibility. It is not about rejecting help or collaboration, but understanding that our success primarily depends on our own efforts and our ability to act independently.

- o **Avoid dependency:** Relying on others for essential tasks can create harmful dependency. It is crucial to develop the skills necessary to achieve our goals without constantly depending on others.

Personal Development

- o **Invest in yourself:** To build a life of wealth, invest in yourself, whether through education, ongoing training, or developing new skills. These investments enable us to achieve our ambitions on our own.

o **Cultivate discipline:** Wealth requires rigorous personal discipline. Perseverance and consistency in work are the pillars that support a prosperous life.

2. **Collaboration: A Complement, Not a Dependency: Strategic Partnerships**

o **Choose effective collaborations:** Collaboration should be viewed as a strategic tool rather than an essential support. Working with others can multiply opportunities and resources but should never replace our own commitment.

o **Share common visions:** The best collaborations are those that align shared visions and goals, creating synergy that goes beyond mere task-sharing.

Contribute and Receive

o **Bring value:** In any collaboration, it is crucial to add value. The more we contribute, the more respect and influence we gain, which enhances our independence.

o **Balance giving and receiving:** A healthy collaboration is a fair exchange where each party contributes something valuable. By giving as much as we receive, we establish balanced and beneficial working relationships.

3. **Determination and Resilience: Keys to Success: Develop a Resilience Mindset**

   o **Face obstacles:** The path to wealth is fraught with challenges. It is our resilience, our ability to overcome challenges, that determines our success. Each failure is a lesson, each obstacle an opportunity for growth.

   o **Stay determined despite difficulties:** Determination allows us to continue moving forward, even when things get tough. It is fueled by a clear vision of our goals and an unwavering commitment to achieving them.

Continuous Work as a Method

- **Adopt a Strong Work Ethic:** Sustainable wealth is not built overnight. It results from constant work, continuous improvement, and sustained effort. One must be prepared to work hard day after day to build a life of prosperity.

- **Adapt and Evolve:** In a perpetually changing world, staying adaptable is crucial. The ability to evolve with changes, to learn and adjust, is essential to maintaining and increasing our wealth.

Conclusion

A truly wealthy life relies on our ability to free ourselves from dependence on others to accomplish what we are supposed to do ourselves. Collaboration is valuable, but the foundation of our success lies in our personal determination and resilience, forged through continuous and dedicated work. By developing our autonomy, investing in ourselves, and cultivating a strong work ethic, we lay the foundation for a life of enduring wealth and prosperity.

Wealth Requires Self and Activity Organization

The pursuit of wealth is a demanding path, requiring more than mere desires or ambitions. It necessitates rigorous organization of oneself and one's activities. It is no coincidence that the most prosperous individuals are often the most organized. They have learned to structure their lives and actions to maximize their efficiency and achieve their goals. Here's why organization is crucial for creating wealth.

1. Personal Organization: Time Management

- **Prioritize Tasks:** Identifying and completing the most important tasks first is essential. This allows you to focus your efforts on what has the most impact.

- **Planning and Scheduling:** A well-defined schedule helps avoid procrastination and ensures that each day is productive. Blocking out time for specific tasks helps maintain constant focus.

Develop Routines

- **Productive Habits:** Daily habits such as reading, exercising, and reflecting build a solid foundation for success. They reinforce discipline and help you stay focused on long-term goals.

- o **Self-Evaluation:** Taking time to review your progress and adjust strategies is crucial. It helps you stay on track and adapt to inevitable changes.

2. Activity Organization: Resource Management

- o **Financial Optimization:** Keeping accurate accounts, budgeting expenses, and investing wisely are essential practices. Good financial management is the cornerstone of wealth accumulation.

- o **Using Tools:** Leveraging technology and project management tools can significantly enhance efficiency. They help track tasks, manage deadlines, and coordinate efforts.

Establish Clear Goals

- o **SMART Goals:** Goals should be Specific, Measurable, Achievable, Relevant, and Time-bound. This provides clear direction and allows for concrete progress measurement.

- o **Long-Term Vision:** Having a clear vision of what you want to accomplish long-term guides daily decisions and aligns efforts toward a common goal.

3. The Importance of Discipline and Consistency: Staying on Course

- o **Avoid Distractions:** In a world full of distractions, it is essential to stay focused on your priorities. Knowing when to say no to things that do not serve your goals is crucial.

- o **Persevere Despite Obstacles:** The road to wealth is rarely linear. Resilience in facing challenges and the ability to persevere are indispensable qualities.

Tracking and Adjusting

- o **Regular Evaluation:** Periodically reevaluating your strategies and actions helps identify what works and what doesn't. This allows for necessary adjustments to stay on track.

- o **Continuous Learning:** Engaging in constant learning, whether acquiring new skills or new information, helps you stay competitive and adaptable.

Wealth is not merely the result of opportunities or talents but also of the organized and methodical management of oneself and one's activities. By developing productive routines, efficiently using resources, setting clear goals, and maintaining rigorous discipline, you maximize your chances of success. Organization is the thread that ties together all the necessary elements for creating and sustaining wealth. By adopting these principles, anyone can transform their aspirations into tangible reality.

Enjoying Self-Discipline

Self-discipline is often perceived as a constraint, a necessary but unpleasant effort to achieve goals. However, it is possible to transform this perception by finding pleasure in the act of self-discipline itself. By adopting a positive approach and focusing on the benefits and satisfactions that self-discipline provides, one can not only improve productivity but also enhance personal well-being. Here's how to enjoy self-discipline.

1. **Understanding the Benefits of Self-Discipline: Achievement and Satisfaction**

   o **Goal Achievement:** The joy and satisfaction experienced when achieving goals through rigorous self-discipline are unparalleled. Each accomplished task reinforces the feeling of competence and self-mastery.

   o **Increased Self-Confidence:** By keeping commitments to yourself, you build greater confidence in your abilities. This confidence boosts motivation and the desire to persist.

Well-Being and Balance

   o **Stress Reduction:** Good organization and effective time management reduce stress and anxiety related to deadlines and responsibilities. Knowing you have control over your life brings inner peace.

o **Health Improvement:** Personal discipline that includes healthy habits like regular exercise and balanced nutrition leads to better physical and mental health.

2. **Making Self-Discipline Enjoyable:** Incorporate Rewarding Activities

o **Personal Rewards:** After completing a challenging task, granting yourself a small reward can make the process more enjoyable. This could be something simple like taking time for a hobby or enjoying your favorite treat.

o **Pleasure in the Activity:** Finding enjoyable aspects in tasks themselves, such as listening to music while working or turning a task into a game, can make self-discipline more pleasant.

Adopt a Positive Attitude

o **Change Perspective:** Rather than viewing self-discipline as an obligation, consider it an opportunity for personal growth and development. This shift in perspective can transform the experience.

o **Celebrate Achievements:** Recognizing and celebrating your progress, even small ones, reinforces motivation and makes the journey more enjoyable.

3. **Creating Positive Habits:** Routine Development

o **Daily Rituals:** Establishing daily rituals that bring joy, such as a morning meditation session or an evening walk, can structure the day in a pleasant way.

- o **Consistency and Repetition:** Repeating small disciplined actions each day creates positive habits that become natural and less burdensome over time.

Tracking and Progress

Keep a Journal: Recording progress and feelings in a journal can help track evolution and stay motivated. It's also an excellent way to recall past successes and anticipate new challenges.

Regular Self-Evaluation: Taking time to reflect on what works and what can be improved keeps you aligned with your goals and allows for necessary adjustments.

Finding pleasure in self-discipline is a matter of attitude and approach. By focusing on tangible benefits and incorporating enjoyable elements into the process, self-discipline can become a source of joy and satisfaction. It is by finding pleasure in small daily victories and adopting a positive perspective that one can truly appreciate the transformative power of self-discipline. Ultimately, this approach leads to a more balanced, fulfilling, and accomplishment-rich life.

The Power of Words as a Remedy for Resentment

Words are a powerful tool, capable of transforming our lives and healing our inner wounds. When used constructively, they can become a remedy for resentment and many other ailments. If you lack resilience, discipline, leadership, or decision-making ability, repeating positive affirmations can trigger profound changes within you.

The Positive Affirmations Method

Creating New Habits

- **Resilience:** If you lack resilience, repeat several times a day for several days, "I am resilient." This affirmation will embed the belief in your ability to overcome challenges.

- **Discipline:** If you are undisciplined, tell yourself daily, "I am very disciplined." This constant repetition will foster a new approach to tasks and responsibilities.

- **Leadership:** If you lack leadership, repeat, "I am a leader." By affirming this, you will begin to embody the qualities of a true leader.

- **Decision Making:** If you struggle with decision-making, say, "I decide quickly and act immediately." This affirmation will help strengthen your confidence in your decision-making abilities.

The Power of Words on Habit Formation

Triggering Action

Repeating positive affirmations is not merely a motivational exercise; it has the power to trigger action. By affirming yourself daily, you program your mind to adopt new behaviors. Each small action you undertake, inspired by these affirmations, contributes to the creation of new habits.

Progressive Transformation

- **Consistency and Perseverance:** Repeat these affirmations for several days, weeks, or even months. Consistency and perseverance are the keys to success.

- **Formation of New Habits:** Each affirmation, repeated and practiced daily, will become a new habit. Over time, these habits will solidify and become an integral part of your personality.

Benefits of Positive Affirmations

Self-Improvement

- **Boosting Self-Esteem:** By affirming yourself positively, you enhance your self-esteem and develop a positive self-image.

- **Reducing Stress and Resentment:** By adopting positive

affirmations, you transform negative thoughts and reduce stress and resentment.

Personal Development

- **Ongoing Growth:** Positive affirmations encourage continuous personal development. They drive you to constantly seek improvement and overcome obstacles.

- **Overall Fulfillment:** By integrating these new habits, you achieve overall fulfillment, both personally and professionally.

The power of words is undeniable. When used correctly, they can be a remedy for resentment and many other personal challenges. By repeating positive affirmations daily, you trigger actions that, over time, transform into new habits. These new habits enhance your resilience, discipline, leadership, and decision-making ability, leading to profound and lasting transformation in your life. Embrace this practice today and discover the transformative power of words in your existence.

Wealth and the Power of Generosity

Wealth, often perceived as the accumulation of material riches, takes on a much deeper dimension when associated with generosity. True wealth is not measured solely in terms of possessions but also by the capacity to give and enrich the lives of others. Generosity, far from depleting our resources, significantly amplifies them.

Generosity: A Key to Prosperity

Creating a Cycle of Giving and Receiving

- **Law of Abundance:** Generosity activates the law of abundance. When we give selflessly, we open the doors to a multitude of blessings that return to us in unexpected ways.

- **Positive Energy:** Giving creates positive energy that attracts further prosperity. This energy fosters an environment conducive to personal and financial growth.

The Transformative Power of Giving

Social Impact

- **Social Impact:** Generosity has a profound impact on society. By sharing our resources, we contribute to improving the living conditions of others, thereby strengthening the social fabric and creating stronger, more united communities.

- **Personal Fulfillment:** Giving provides a deep sense of satisfaction and happiness. This inner joy enhances our well-being and personal growth.

Generosity as an Investment

Investing in Others

- **Human Capital:** By investing in the education, health, and well-being of others, we develop human capital that is essential for collective progress. The returns on this investment are invaluable and enduring.

- **Networks and Relationships:** Generosity forges strong and lasting relationships. The people we help today can become valuable allies tomorrow, creating a network of support and mutual cooperation.

Giving to Grow

- **Expansion of Awareness:** Generosity opens us to new perspectives and experiences. It broadens our awareness and helps us understand the importance of human interconnectedness.

- **Skill Development:** By giving our time, talents, and resources, we develop leadership, management, and communication skills, which are crucial for our personal and professional success.

The Multiple Benefits of Generosity

Health and Well-Being

- **Stress Reduction:** Generosity reduces stress and promotes better mental health. Acts of kindness release endorphins, creating a sense of well-being.

- **Longevity:** Studies show that generous people tend to live longer and lead more fulfilling lives.

Success and Achievement

- **Attraction of Opportunities:** Generous acts attract opportunities. People are naturally inclined to support and partner with those who give without expecting anything in return.

- **Reputation and Influence:** Generosity builds a solid and respected reputation. It enhances our influence and ability to inspire others.

True wealth is not merely in the accumulation of material possessions but in the power of generosity. By giving freely and generously, we create a cycle of prosperity and abundance that enriches our lives and those of others. Generosity transforms our existence, opens us to new opportunities, and enhances our well-being. Let us embrace generosity as a guiding principle and discover the phenomenal impact it can have on our wealth and power.

The Importance of Peaceful Rest

Balance and Well-being

- **Mental Health:** Peaceful rest is essential for maintaining good mental health. It helps reduce stress, decrease anxiety, and foster a positive attitude towards life's challenges.

- **Physical Health:** Restorative sleep and regular relaxation strengthen the immune system, increase energy, and improve longevity. The combination of wealth and health constitutes invaluable richness.

Mental Clarity and Creativity

- **Informed Decisions:** A rested mind is capable of making more informed and strategic decisions. Mental tranquility allows for discerning evaluation of situations and wise choices.

- **Innovation:** Rest stimulates creativity. Moments of calm and relaxation often lead to the emergence of new ideas and innovative solutions.

Integrating Rest into the Pursuit of Wealth

- **Planning and Time Management:**

  o **Prioritizing Rest:** Incorporating periods of rest and relaxation into our schedules is crucial. Planning for moments of calm helps recharge our batteries and increase long-term productivity.

  o **Effective Time Management:** Using time management

techniques, such as the Pomodoro method or block planning, helps balance intense work periods with rest.

Cultivating Mindfulness

- o **Meditation and Breathing:** Practicing meditation and mindful breathing helps calm the mind and find inner peace. These techniques are powerful tools for integrating peaceful rest into our daily lives.

- o **Presence and Awareness:** Being fully present in each moment, whether at work or in relaxation, enhances our ability to appreciate life and find a harmonious balance.

Benefits of Peaceful Rest

- **Increased Productivity:** A rested mind and body function optimally, thereby increasing productivity and efficiency in our professional activities.

- **Quality of Work:** Peaceful rest improves the quality of our work. We become more attentive, focused, and capable of producing exceptional results.

Personal Fulfillment

- **Satisfaction and Happiness:** The combination of wealth and peaceful rest leads to a fulfilled and happy life. We are able to savor our successes and fully enjoy life's simple pleasures.

- **Harmonious Relationships:** A peaceful mind fosters more harmonious and balanced relationships. We become more patient, understanding, and capable of giving and receiving love.

True wealth is not limited to material possessions but also includes peaceful rest, that state of inner tranquility that allows us to fully enjoy our achievements. By integrating peaceful rest into our pursuit of wealth, we create a harmonious balance that nurtures our well-being and happiness. The combination of wealth and peaceful rest constitutes complete and enduring richness, enabling us to lead a fulfilled and satisfying life.

Seeing Fortune for Others

In our personal quest for success and prosperity, it is crucial to remember the importance of kindness and generosity towards others. Seeing fortune for others means recognizing and encouraging everyone's potential to achieve wealth, not only material but also emotional and spiritual. It is a philosophy that transcends selfishness and creates a virtuous cycle of shared prosperity.

The Impact of Seeing Fortune for Others

- **Strengthening Social Bonds:** By wishing and working for the fortune of others, we strengthen the ties within our community. A supportive community is more resilient and able to overcome challenges together.

- **Reducing Inequality:** Encouraging fortune for others helps reduce inequality. It creates opportunities for those who are less fortunate and promotes a more equitable distribution of resources.

Creating a Positive Environment

- **Atmosphere of Kindness:** A positive and generous attitude towards others creates an atmosphere of kindness and mutual support. This inspires and motivates people to give their best.

- **Ripple Effect:** Generosity and kindness are contagious. By seeing fortune for others, we trigger a ripple effect where everyone is inspired to help and support each other, creating a virtuous circle of prosperity.

How to See Fortune for Others

- **Encouragement and Support:**

  o **Recognize Potentials:** Take time to recognize and encourage others' talents and skills. This motivates them to pursue their goals and realize their potential.

  o **Offer Opportunities:** Create and offer opportunities for others, whether through mentoring, training, or simply sharing resources and knowledge.

Acts of Generosity

  o **Giving Time:** Offer time to help others with their projects or to support them during difficult times. Time is a precious resource that can make a significant difference.

  o **Sharing Resources:** Share material and immaterial resources, such as books, professional contacts, or even valuable advice.

Benefits of Seeing Fortune for Others

  o **Personal and Collective Prosperity:** Generosity and altruism enrich our lives in immeasurable ways. They bring a deep satisfaction and joy that cannot be measured in monetary terms.

- o **Collective Growth:** When we see fortune for others, we contribute to collective growth. A society where everyone prospers is stronger, more innovative, and more dynamic.

Emotional and Spiritual Well-being

- **Inner Fulfillment:** The satisfaction of seeing others succeed and thrive brings a sense of peace and inner happiness. It is a form of spiritual wealth that nourishes our soul.

- **Harmony and Peace:** A benevolent attitude towards others fosters harmonious and peaceful relationships. It reduces conflicts and creates an environment of mutual respect and understanding.

Seeing fortune for others is a powerful philosophy that enriches not only those we help but also our own lives. By recognizing and encouraging the potential in others, we create a more just, equitable, and prosperous society. Generosity and kindness have a profound and lasting impact, transforming not only individual lives but also the community as a whole. Let us adopt this vision of fortune for others and contribute to creating a world where everyone has the opportunity to thrive.

How to Sell Your Ideas

Selling your ideas is a crucial skill for transforming your creativity into tangible success. Whether you want to launch a business, persuade investors, or influence decision-makers, here are key strategies for effectively selling your ideas:

1. **Develop a Clear Value Proposition**

    o **Identify the Problem:** Start by clearly identifying the problem your idea solves. Understanding the needs of your target audience is crucial.

    o **Unique Solution:** Describe how your idea offers a unique or innovative solution. Highlight what sets it apart from existing solutions.

    o **Concrete Benefits:** List the tangible benefits your idea brings, whether in terms of saving time, money, productivity, or quality of life.

2. **Know Your Audience**

    o **Research and Segmentation:** Know your target audience. Conduct research to understand their needs, desires, and concerns.

    o **Personalization:** Tailor your message to your audience. What works for investors may not be effective for potential customers.

3. **Create a Powerful Pitch**

o **Clear Structure:** A good pitch should have a clear structure: introduction, problem, solution, benefits, and conclusion.

o **Storytelling:** Use stories to make your idea more memorable and engaging. Share anecdotes or concrete examples that illustrate the impact of your idea.

o **Impactful Visuals:** Use visuals, graphics, and demonstrations to make your presentation more appealing and understandable.

4. **Build Trust and Credibility**

o **Proofs and Testimonials:** Use tangible proofs such as case studies, customer testimonials, market data, and prototypes to enhance the credibility of your idea.

o **Expertise:** Highlight your expertise and that of your team. Show that you have the skills and knowledge necessary to implement your idea.

5. **Use Appropriate Communication Channels**

o **Presentations and Meetings:** Face-to-face presentations or online meetings are ideal for interactive dialogue.

o **Social Media:** Use social media to share your idea and attract attention. Platforms like LinkedIn, Twitter, and

Facebook can be very effective.

- o **Publications and Media:** Write blog posts, white papers, or articles in specialized magazines to reach a wider audience and establish your authority.

6. **Engage and Follow Up**

- o **Interactivity:** Engage your audience by asking questions, soliciting feedback, and encouraging discussions.

- o **Regular Follow-up:** After your presentation or pitch, ensure regular follow-up. Answer questions, provide additional information, and maintain contact.

7. **Adapt and Refine**

- o **Feedback:** Be receptive to feedback and willing to adjust your idea based on constructive criticism.

- o **Continuous Improvement:** Continuously refine your pitch and value proposition to better meet the expectations and needs of your audience.

Selling your ideas requires a combination of clarity, persuasion, and strategy. By understanding your audience, developing a compelling value proposition, and using the right communication channels, you can maximize your chances of success. Remember that perseverance and continuous improvement are essential to turning your ideas into profitable realities.

How to Access the World of Ideas

Accessing the world of ideas requires an open mind, curiosity, and a systematic approach to stimulate creativity. Here are some strategies to help you enter this fascinating world and generate innovative ideas:

1. **Cultivate Curiosity**

   - **Ask Questions:** Adopt a constant questioning attitude. Ask questions about everything around you. Why are things the way they are? How could they be improved?

   - **Explore New Topics:** Don't limit yourself to your usual fields of expertise. Read books, watch documentaries, and take online courses on a variety of subjects to broaden your horizon.

2. **Create a Stimulating Environment**

   - **Inspiring Workspace:** Design a workspace that stimulates your creativity, with colors, objects, and artwork that inspire you.

   - **Avoid Distractions:** Reduce distractions by limiting access to electronic devices and creating time slots dedicated to reflection and creativity.

3. **Practice Meditation and Mindfulness**

   - **Meditation:** Meditation helps clarify the mind and improve concentration, creating a space conducive to the emergence of new ideas.

o **Mindfulness:** Practicing mindfulness by being attentive to the present moment can help you better observe and understand your environment, thus fostering idea generation.

4. **Use Brainstorming Techniques**

o **Individual Brainstorming:** Write down all the ideas that come to mind without judgment. Let your imagination run wild.

o **Collective Brainstorming:** Collaborate with others to stimulate collective creativity. Interactions and exchanges can trigger ideas you might not have had alone.

5. **Read and Write Regularly**

o **Reading:** Read books, articles, and blogs to expose yourself to new ideas and perspectives. Reading activates your brain and can inspire new thoughts.

o **Writing:** Keep an idea journal where you record all your thoughts, reflections, and inspirations. Writing can help clarify and develop your ideas.

6. **Step Out of Your Comfort Zone**

o **New Experiences:** Participate in new and varied activities, whether traveling, taking courses, or engaging in hobbies. Breaking your routine can stimulate creativity.

o **Meet New People:** Engage in conversations with people from different backgrounds and cultures. Interacting with diverse perspectives can enrich your own thinking.

7. **Use Creativity Tools and Techniques**

o **Mind Mapping:** Use mind maps to visually organize your ideas and see connections between them.

o **Lateral Thinking Techniques:** Learn techniques such as reverse brainstorming or the six thinking hats method to approach problems from different angles.

8. **Learn from Failure**

o **See Failure as Opportunity:** View each failure as a learning opportunity. Analyze what went wrong and use those lessons to generate new ideas.

o **Perseverance:** Don't get discouraged by obstacles. Perseverance is often key to accessing revolutionary ideas.

Accessing the world of ideas requires a combination of curiosity, deliberate practices, and openness to new experiences. By cultivating an open mind, creating a conducive environment for reflection, and using specific techniques to stimulate creativity, you can tap into the vast reservoir of ideas around you. Whether through reading, meditation, brainstorming, or exploring new activities, each action you take can bring you closer to the emergence of new ideas.

All the Riches of the World Are Your Inheritance

It is essential to understand that each individual possesses within them the potential to access infinite riches. These riches are not limited to material possessions but also include the wealth of the mind, heart, and soul. By recognizing and embracing this potential, we can transform our lives and the lives of others in significant ways.

1. Inner Wealth

    o **Wisdom and Knowledge:** Knowledge is an invaluable treasure. By continuously cultivating our minds through learning and experimentation, we develop a deep understanding of the world around us.

    o **Creativity and Imagination:** Creativity is an inexhaustible source of riches. By letting our imagination run free, we can come up with innovative ideas and unique solutions to the challenges we face.

2. Emotional Wealth

    o **Love and Compassion:** Love and compassion enrich our relationships and bring profound emotional satisfaction. By giving and receiving love, we create a harmonious and joyful environment.

o **Resilience and Optimism:** Cultivating a positive attitude and strong resilience in the face of adversity is crucial. These qualities allow us to overcome obstacles and see opportunities even in difficult times.

3. **Material Wealth**

o **Financial Abundance:** Intelligent management of our finances, investing in promising opportunities, and creating diversified sources of income are ways to increase our material wealth.

o **Possessions and Comfort:** Material goods, when used wisely, can enhance our quality of life and provide comfort. However, it is important not to let them define our personal values.

4. **Social Wealth**

o **Network and Connections:** The relationships we cultivate with others can open doors and create unexpected opportunities. A strong network of contacts is a valuable asset.

o **Contributions and Impact:** By sharing our wealth, whether material, intellectual, or emotional, we also enrich the lives of others. The positive impact we have on the world is a form of wealth in itself.

5. **Spiritual Wealth**

o **Inner Peace:** The quest for inner peace and harmony with oneself is the supreme form of wealth. It allows us to live in accordance with our values and find a deep sense of purpose in our existence.

o **Connection with the Universe:** By recognizing our connection with the universe and aligning our actions with our life mission, we attract positive energies and opportunities that further enrich us.

All the riches of the world are within our reach as an innate inheritance of our humanity. By cultivating different forms of wealth—inner, emotional, material, social, and spiritual—we can lead a fulfilling and abundant life. It is our responsibility to recognize this potential within us and use it not only to enrich our own lives but also to benefit those around us. By embracing this holistic view of wealth, we can truly realize our full potential and live a life of prosperity and fulfillment.

Destined to Prosper and Live in Peace in an Illusory World

It is crucial to understand that our existence on this Earth goes far beyond mere survival and paying bills. We are destined for greater achievements: to prosper, live in peace, and transcend the illusions of this material world.

1. **Vision of Greatness**

o **High Goals:** We have within us the capacity to aim high and achieve grand dreams. The limits we perceive are often mental constructs. By adopting a vision of greatness, we give ourselves permission to aim beyond the mere necessities of life.

o **Ambition and Determination:** The combination of ambition and determination is essential for turning our aspirations into realities. It is not enough to dream big; we must also work with perseverance to achieve our goals.

2. **Prospering**

o **Abundance Mentality:** Adopting an abundance mentality means believing that there is enough wealth for everyone. By changing our perspective on money and wealth, we can attract more prosperity into our lives.

- **Value Creation:** True prosperity comes from creating value for others. Whether through innovation, entrepreneurship, or service, by offering something meaningful to the world, we also enrich ourselves.

- **Smart Investment:** Wisely managing our financial resources and investing in profitable opportunities helps us build lasting wealth. Financial education and informed decision-making are key skills in this process.

3. **Living in Peace**

- **Inner Peace:** True peace begins within us. By cultivating tranquility through meditation, reflection, and gratitude practice, we can navigate this world with serenity.

- **Life Balance:** Living in peace involves finding a balance between different aspects of our lives—work, relationships, health, and personal growth. This balance allows us to fully enjoy our material success without sacrificing our well-being.

4. **Transcending the Illusory World**

- **Awakened Awareness:** Recognizing that this material world is often an illusion helps us avoid being trapped by superficial desires. Awakened awareness allows us to see beyond appearances and seek deeper truths.

- **Spiritual Alignment:** By aligning our actions with our

spiritual values, we can live an authentic and meaningful life. This alignment guides us toward choices that nourish our souls rather than merely satisfying material needs.

We are not destined merely to pay bills and survive. Our true destiny is to prosper, live in peace, and transcend the illusions of the material world. By embracing a vision of greatness, creating value, investing wisely, and cultivating inner peace, we can realize our full potential. Ultimately, living a life of abundance and serenity is not only possible but also our right and inheritance.

Claim Your Fortune Now

It is time to understand and accept that wealth and abundance are within your reach, here and now. Returning to the source of your potential and taking the necessary steps to claim your right to prosperity is essential for transforming your life.

1. **Recognize Your Value**

o **Self-Esteem:** The first step to claiming your fortune is to recognize your own value. You have unique talents, skills, and qualities that set you apart. Become aware of your potential and have confidence in yourself.

o **Positive Beliefs:** Change your limiting beliefs into positive affirmations. Believe in your ability to attract wealth and abundance. Tell yourself daily: "I deserve wealth" and "Prosperity belongs to me."

2. **Adopt an Abundance Mentality**

o **Visualization:** Use visualization to see and feel the life of your dreams. Imagine yourself surrounded by wealth, success, and happiness. This practice will help attract these elements into your reality.

o **Gratitude:** Cultivate gratitude for what you already have. Recognizing and appreciating your current blessings attracts more positive things into your life.

3. **Take Concrete Actions**

o **Set Goals:** Define clear and specific goals for what you wish to achieve. Whether it's a certain level of income, an entrepreneurial project, or investments, having precise goals gives you clear direction.

o **Strategic Planning:** Create an action plan to achieve your goals. Identify the necessary steps and follow them with determination. Claiming your fortune requires a plan and methodical execution.

4. **Develop Financial Skills**

o **Financial Education:** Take time to educate yourself about personal finance, investments, and money management. Understanding how money works is crucial for attracting and maintaining wealth.

o **Smart Investments:** Learn to identify and seize investment opportunities. Whether in the stock market, real estate, or businesses, wise investments can multiply your resources.

5. **Create Value**

o **Innovation and Creativity:** Use your creativity to find innovative ways to create value for others. The more value you provide, the more you receive in return.

o   **Entrepreneurship:** Consider entrepreneurship as a way to claim your fortune. Starting your own business can be a powerful path to achieving your financial aspirations.

6. **Maintain a Positive Attitude**

o   **Resilience:** Show resilience in the face of challenges. The path to fortune is not always easy, but your ability to persevere will determine your success.

o   **Optimism:** Adopt an optimistic attitude. Believing in a bright future and being positive attracts opportunities and people who can help you achieve your ambitions.

Claiming your fortune is a process that starts with recognizing your own value and transforming your mindset. By taking concrete actions, educating yourself financially, and creating value, you can attract the abundance you deserve. Never forget that fortune and prosperity are your birthright. It is time to claim them now and live the life of your dreams.

Stay Relaxed and Grateful When Everything Goes Awry

Life is a series of ups and downs, moments of success, and unexpected challenges. It is easy to feel overwhelmed when everything seems to go wrong. Yet, there is a powerful and soothing approach: staying calm and practicing gratitude, even in difficult times. Here's how:

1. Accept Uncertainty

   o **Understand Impermanence:** Life is inherently changeable. Accepting that everything is temporary helps to put difficult moments into perspective. Remember that "this too shall pass."

   o **Live in the Present Moment:** Focus on the present moment. Often, anxiety comes from concerns about the past or future. Practicing mindfulness can help you stay grounded in the present.

2. Practice Gratitude

   o **Recognize Small Blessings:** Even when everything seems to go wrong, there is always something to be grateful for. Identify these small blessings and give thanks for them.

   o **Keep a Gratitude Journal:** Write down three things you

are grateful for each day. This can shift your perspective and help you see the light in dark times.

3. **Adopt a Relaxed Attitude**

o **Deep Breathing:** Use deep breathing techniques to calm your mind and reduce stress. A few minutes of conscious breathing can make a significant difference.

o **Meditation:** Meditation is a powerful tool for soothing the mind and strengthening resilience in the face of difficulties. Incorporate it into your daily routine.

4. **Trust the Process**

o **Faith in a Greater Plan:** Believing that each experience, even difficult ones, is part of a greater plan can provide comfort. This perspective can transform challenges into learning opportunities.

o **Resilience and Growth:** Remember that difficult moments are often those that help us grow the most. Trust in your ability to overcome obstacles and emerge stronger.

5. **Cultivate Positive Relationships**

o **Support from Loved Ones:** Surround yourself with positive and encouraging people. Talking to a friend or family member can provide crucial emotional support.

o **Support Networks:** Join support groups or communities

with shared interests to gain a sense of belonging and encouragement.

6. **Learn and Adapt**

o **Life Lessons:** Each challenge brings with it a valuable lesson. Identify what you can learn from the current situation and how it can help you grow.

o **Flexibility and Adaptability:** Being flexible and willing to adapt to changes can turn negative situations into enriching experiences.

When everything seems to be going wrong, it is crucial to stay calm, breathe deeply, and remember the small things you can be grateful for. Adopting an attitude of gratitude and relaxation in the face of adversity can not only soothe the mind but also pave the way for unexpected solutions and personal growth. Ultimately, staying serene and grateful transforms challenges into opportunities and enriches our life experience.

Master Your Wealth

Wealth is not limited to financial abundance; it also encompasses fulfillment in all aspects of life. To truly master your wealth, adopt a holistic approach that embraces physical, mental, emotional, and financial well-being. Here's how:

1. **Define Your Vision of Wealth**

   o **Clarity of Goals:** Identify what wealth means to you. Is it financial freedom, happiness, personal growth, or a combination of these?

   o **Creative Visualization:** Imagine living the life of your dreams. Visualize each detail with clarity and conviction to strengthen your desire to succeed.

2. **Take Concrete Steps**

   o **Financial Planning:** Establish a solid financial plan that includes saving, investing, and managing debt. Consult financial experts if necessary to help you develop a strategy suited to your goals.

   o **Personal Development:** Invest in your personal growth by reading books, taking courses, and practicing skills that enhance your self-confidence and ability to succeed.

3. **Cultivate a Prosperity Mindset**

o **Positive Thinking:** Adopt a positive attitude toward money and wealth. Firmly believe in your ability to attract abundance into your life.

o **Daily Gratitude:** Practice gratitude for what you already have while aspiring for more. Gratitude opens the door to new opportunities and strengthens your connection with universal abundance.

4. **Manage Your Resources Wisely**

o **Work-Life Balance:** Prioritize your health and well-being by taking time to rest, recharge, and enjoy life outside of work.

o **Invest in Relationships:** Cultivate meaningful relationships with family, friends, and your community. Enriching relationships contributes to your overall well-being and sense of wealth.

5. **Be Open to Opportunities**

o **Flexibility and Adaptability:** Stay open to changes and opportunities that come your way. Sometimes, the least expected paths lead to the greatest rewards.

o **Learn from Failure:** Do not fear failure but see it as an opportunity to learn and grow. Lessons learned from setbacks can propel you to new heights of success.

6. **Share Your Wealth with the World**

o **Philanthropy:** Look for ways to give back to the community and help those who are less fortunate. Generosity creates a virtuous circle of abundance and gratitude.

o **Sharing Knowledge:** Share your knowledge and experience with others to help them achieve their own goals of wealth and success.

Mastering your wealth goes beyond simply accumulating material possessions. It means creating a balanced and fulfilling life in all aspects, including financial, personal, and relational. By clearly defining your goals, taking concrete steps, and cultivating a prosperous mindset, you can reach new heights of success and satisfaction in your life. True wealth lies in the ability to live fully and contribute positively to the world around us.

Your wealth extends beyond what you see.

Your Riches Exceed Appearances

Beyond material possessions and tangible assets lie much deeper and more meaningful treasures. Here's how to discover and cultivate these inner riches:

1. **The Riches of the Mind**

   o **Accumulated Wisdom:** Your mind is an inexhaustible reservoir of knowledge and experience. Cultivate curiosity and continuous learning to enrich your mind day by day.

   o **Unlimited Creativity:** Your ability to create, imagine, and innovate is an invaluable wealth. Explore your creative talents and use them to shape a better world around you.

2. **The Riches of Relationships**

   o **Deep Connections:** Authentic and meaningful relationships with others are precious treasures. Invest time and energy in your relationships to cultivate lasting and enriching connections.

   o **Sharing Love:** The love and affection you share with your family, friends, and community are an infinite source of wealth. Nourish these bonds with care and compassion.

3. **The Riches of Health**

   o **Holistic Well-being:** Physical, mental, and emotional

health is the foundation of all true wealth. Take care of your body and mind by adopting healthy and balanced lifestyle habits.

o   **Thriving Vitality:** The vitality and energy you feel when you are healthy are valuable riches that allow you to fully enjoy life and achieve your goals.

4. The Riches of Experience

o   **Lessons Learned:** Every experience, whether positive or negative, is an opportunity for learning and growth. Gather the insights from your past experiences to evolve and continuously improve.

o   **Acquired Wisdom:** Over time, you accumulate valuable wisdom that guides your choices and decisions. Trust your intuition and discernment to navigate life confidently.

5. The Riches of the Soul

o   **Deep Alignment:** When you live in accordance with your values and true self, you experience a deep and enduring inner richness. Seek connection with your soul and follow its call with confidence.

o   **Mindfulness:** Practicing mindfulness and gratitude allows you to fully savor each moment of life, revealing the infinite richness present in the present moment.

Your riches far exceed what the eye can see. By exploring the depths of your mind, cultivating authentic relationships, caring for your health, learning from your experiences, and nurturing your soul, you will discover an abundance that goes well beyond material possessions. Cultivate these inner riches with care and attention, as they bring true fulfillment and profound meaning to your life.

Everything Comes from the Great "I AM": Stop and Know That I Am God

Recognizing the presence of the Great, "I AM" is an invitation to connect with the source of all creation, the universal consciousness that resides within each of us. Here's how to integrate this perspective into your life:

Awakening to the Divine Presence

- **Self-Awareness:** Become aware of your connection with the "I AM," the divine presence within you. By acknowledging this fundamental truth, you realize that you are a unique expression of divinity.

- **Acceptance of Inner Power:** Understand that the power to create, manifest, and transform resides within you, as you are an extension of this universal consciousness. Allow yourself to embrace this power with humility and gratitude.

Co-Creation with the Universe

- **Alignment with Intention:** By harmonizing your thoughts, words, and actions with universal consciousness, you create a powerful alignment that facilitates the manifestation of your deepest desires.

- **Trust in the Universe:** Trust in the infinite intelligence of the universe to guide you on your path. Let go of the need to control every aspect of your life and allow magic to unfold naturally.

Responsibility and Compassion

- **Personal Responsibility:** Recognize that you are the co-creator of your reality and take responsibility for your thoughts, emotions, and actions. Use this awareness to shape a life aligned with your highest values and aspirations.

- **Universal Compassion:** Cultivate compassion towards yourself and others, acknowledging that we are all expressions of the same divine source. Treat yourself and others with love and respect, honoring the divinity within each.

Reverence for Life

- **Infinite Gratitude:** Express deep gratitude for every aspect of your life, recognizing that each experience, whether positive or negative, is an opportunity for learning and growth.

- **Celebration of Existence:** Live each moment with wonder and joy, knowing that you are fully immersed in the flow of life. Elevate your awareness to see the beauty and perfection that surround you, even in the simplest moments.

By recognizing the presence of the Great "I AM" within you, you realize your divine nature and unlimited potential as a co-creator of your reality. With this awakened consciousness, you can navigate life confidently, knowing that you are supported by the infinite intelligence of the universe. May this sacred truth inspire you to fully embrace your power and manifest your highest destiny in this world and beyond.

Every Excellent Gift Comes from Above

Recognizing that every excellent gift comes from above is an act of gratitude and humility toward the source of all blessings. Here's how to integrate this perspective into your life:

Acknowledgment of the Source

- **Universal Gratitude:** Express profound gratitude to the source of all grace, acknowledging that every blessing, opportunity, and success is a precious gift given to us.

- **Humility Before Greatness:** Cultivate humility by recognizing that our achievements and blessings are not solely the result of our efforts but are the result of divine grace granted to us.

Alignment with Divine Will

- **Inner Listening:** Learn to listen to the voice of inner wisdom, guiding your steps on the path of truth and light. By aligning your will with divine will, you open the way to manifesting your highest potential.

- **Acceptance of Challenges:** Accept challenges and trials with faith and resilience, knowing that even in the most difficult moments, you are supported by divine grace that strengthens and guides you.

Sharing the Blessing

- **Generosity and Compassion:** Share the blessings you have received with generosity and compassion towards others. By offering your love and support, you become a channel of grace for those in need.

- **Selfless Service:** Engage in acts of selfless service, offering your time, talents, and resources for the well-being of others. By serving others with love and dedication, you reflect the divine grace flowing through you.

Unshakable Faith

- **Trust in the Invisible:** Have faith in the invisible work of divine grace, knowing that even when circumstances seem dark, you are enveloped by the light and protection of the divine source.

- **Perseverance in Adversity:** Staying strong and persevering in times of difficulty, knowing that each challenge is an opportunity for growth and transformation under the benevolent guidance of divine grace.

By recognizing that every excellent gift comes from above, you open your heart and mind to the infinite abundance of blessings and benefits that surround you. May this awakened awareness inspire you to live each day with gratitude, humility, and faith, knowing that you are loved and supported by the source of all grace in this world and beyond.

Heroic Acts: Big or Small, Everywhere and in Everything

In our daily lives, we all have the opportunity to perform heroic acts, whether big or small. These gestures, often simple but full of compassion and courage, can transform lives and bring positive change to our world. Here are some ideas for incorporating heroic acts into your life, everywhere and in everything:

Everyday Heroes

1. **Offer a Smile:** A simple smile can brighten someone's day. Take the time to smile at others, even strangers, as such a small gesture can spread joy and kindness around you.

2. **Listen with Empathy:** Give a listening ear to those in need. Listening without judgment and with compassion can provide comfort and support to someone in distress.

3. **Help Spontaneously:** Offer your help without waiting to be asked. Whether it's carrying groceries for an elderly person, giving up your seat on public transport, or assisting a struggling colleague, every gesture matters.

Acts of Generosity

1. **Give Your Time:** Engage in volunteer activities. Whether

serving at a soup kitchen, participating in a neighborhood cleanup, or helping at an animal shelter, giving your time is a priceless act of generosity.

2. **Share Resources:** Share what you have with those who have less. Whether it's clothing, food, or even skills, every donation can make a significant difference in someone's life.

3. **Encourage and Inspire:** Take the time to encourage and inspire others. A kind word, a motivating phrase, or a supportive gesture can help someone overcome obstacles and achieve their goals.

Courage and Compassion

1. **Stand Up for the Oppressed:** Have the courage to stand up for those who cannot defend themselves. Whether by denouncing injustice or supporting an important cause, your voice can be a powerful force for good.

2. **Daily Acts of Courage:** Face your fears and step out of your comfort zone. Whether by speaking up for your ideas, undertaking an ambitious project, or confronting a difficult situation, every act of courage strengthens your character.

3. **Sow Peace:** Choose peace in your daily interactions. Resolve conflicts with calm and understanding, and be an agent of peace and reconciliation in your community.

Heroic acts don't always require grand gestures or spectacular actions. They can manifest in the small things in life, through simple yet compassionate, generous, and courageous acts. Every day is an opportunity to show heroism, inspire others, and contribute to a better world. By showing kindness and performing acts of goodness, big or small, you become an everyday hero, leaving a positive and lasting impact on the world around you.

You Are the Great Hero

In the journey of life, we often look for heroes—those admirable figures who achieve great feats and inspire with their courage and strength. Yet, it is essential to remember that the greatest hero of your life is actually... yourself. Here's why you are the great hero of your own story:

Inner Strength

1. **Overcome Obstacles:** Every challenge you have faced and overcome speaks to your inner strength. Whether professional difficulties, personal problems, or unforeseen trials, your resilience has allowed you to persevere.

2. **Believe in Yourself:** Self-confidence is key to achieving heroic feats. By believing in your abilities and committing to reaching your goals, you prove each day that you are capable of accomplishing extraordinary things.

3. **Rise After Falls:** Failures are an integral part of the heroic journey. What sets a hero apart is the ability to rise after each fall, learn from mistakes, and continue moving forward with determination.

Positive Impact

1. **Inspire Others:** Through your actions, you inspire those

around you. Whether through hard work, kindness, or courage, you have the power to encourage and motivate others to follow your example.

2. **Help with Compassion:** Every act of generosity and compassion you perform contributes to a better world. By helping those in need, you become a source of light and hope for others.

3. **Create Change:** You have the power to effect change. Whether participating in community initiatives, advocating important causes, or making ethical choices, your actions have a real impact on your environment.

Personal Growth

1. **Learn and Grow:** A true hero never stops learning. Every experience, whether positive or negative, is an opportunity to grow and become a better version of yourself.

2. **Listen to Your Heart:** Following your passions and listening to your intuition are heroic acts. By staying true to yourself and your dreams, you lead an authentic and fulfilling life.

3. **Cultivate Gratitude:** Recognizing and appreciating the small and large victories in life enhances your heroism. Gratitude helps you stay positive and value every moment

of your journey.

You are the hero of your own story. Your inner strength, ability to inspire and help others, and commitment to learning and growing make you a heroic figure in your own life. Never forget that each day is a new page of your heroic adventure, and you have the power to create a positive and lasting impact on the world. Be proud of your journey, continue moving forward with courage and determination, and always remember that you are the great hero you seek.

You Are Unique, Powerful, Incomparable, and Indispensable

Each of us possesses qualities and talents that make us unique. In a world where it's easy to compare ourselves to others, it's crucial to remember our own intrinsic value. Here's why you are unique, powerful, incomparable, and indispensable.

Uniqueness

1. **Your Personal Story:** Every life experience, every challenge overcome, and every lesson learned contribute to making you a unique individual. No one else has lived exactly what you have lived, and this shapes a particular perspective and strength.

2. **Your Talents and Skills:** Whether you are an artist, entrepreneur, teacher, or something else, your talents and skills are unique. They are the result of your passions, hard work, and dedication.

3. **Your Essence:** Your way of being, your character, and your values are distinct. They shape your relationships, your work, and your worldview.

Power

1. **The Power of Will:** Your determination and perseverance are powerful forces. They enable you to overcome obstacles and achieve your goals, no matter the difficulties encountered.

2. **The Impact of Actions:** Every action, big or small, has an impact. Your power lies in your ability to choose actions that reflect your values and contribute positively to your life and the lives of others.

3. **Inner Strength:** Your resilience and ability to bounce back after failures are testaments to your inner power. You have the strength to overcome challenges and turn obstacles into opportunities.

Incomparability

1. **Originality:** There is no one else like you. Your ideas, creativity, and way of thinking are original and make a unique contribution to the world.

2. **Personal Value:** Comparing your value to others is unnecessary, as each person has their own path and talents. Recognizing and appreciating your own value allows you to fully thrive.

3. **Authenticity:** By staying true to yourself, you show an

authenticity that cannot be compared. Your authenticity attracts and inspires others, creating deep and meaningful connections.

Indispensability

1. **Positive Influence:** Your actions and choices can positively influence your environment. You are indispensable in creating positive changes in your life and the lives of others.

2. **Presence:** Your presence, whether physical or emotional, has a significant impact. Being present for others and for yourself is an indispensable quality that enriches relationships and experiences.

3. **Unique Contribution:** You bring something unique and irreplaceable to the world. Whether through your work, your love, or your support, your contribution is precious and irreplaceable.

You are unique, powerful, incomparable, and indispensable. By recognizing and embracing these qualities, you can live a fulfilling and authentic life. Celebrate your uniqueness, exercise your power with kindness, appreciate your incomparability, and acknowledge your indispensable nature in the world. You have an immense and irreplaceable impact simply by being yourself.

You Are the Unique and Most Radiant Light

In the vastness of the universe, every human being shines with a light of their own. You are that unique and radiant light, illuminating not only your own path but also that of others. Here's why your light is so precious and how it can transform the world around you.

The uniqueness of Your Light

1. **A Beacon in the Darkness:** Your light, as individual as it is, is a beacon for those around you. It guides, inspires, and brings hope in times of doubt and difficulty.

2. **Personal Brilliance:** No one else possesses the same combination of qualities, talents, and experiences as you. Your light is a reflection of everything that makes you unique, and that's what makes it irreplaceable.

3. **Authenticity:** By staying true to yourself, you allow your true light to shine. Authenticity attracts and inspires others to do the same, creating a virtuous circle of positivity and truth.

Power of Your Radiance

1. **Illuminating Others:** Your light has the power to touch and influence the lives of others profoundly. Through your actions, words, and presence, you bring warmth and clarity to the lives of those around you.

2. **Revealing Hidden Potentials:** Your light helps reveal hidden potentials, both in yourself and in those you touch, by breaking through the darkness of ignorance and fear. It opens doors to new possibilities and realities.

3. **Spreading Positivity:** The light you emit spreads far beyond your own existence. It is reflected in the positive actions you inspire in others, creating a ripple effect of kindness and generosity.

Radiance of Your Light

1. **Beauty and Joy:** A radiant light brings unparalleled beauty and joy. Your presence and energy create an environment where inner and outer beauty can flourish.

2. **Infinite Inspiration:** A light that shines brightly is an inexhaustible source of inspiration. You motivate and encourage others to see the beauty in every moment and aspire to be the best version of themselves.

3. **Courage and Resilience:** Your radiant light shows the path of courage and resilience. It proves that no matter the obstacles, you can always find a way to shine even brighter.

You are the unique and most radiant light. Your brilliance is a powerful force that can transform lives and illuminate the world. By embracing your uniqueness, recognizing the power of your light, and letting your radiance shine, you become a source of beauty, joy, and immeasurable inspiration. Your light is not only a gift to yourself but to everyone fortunate enough to cross your path. Keep shining, for the world needs your light.

Constant Gratitude

Gratitude is a powerful force that transforms our perception of the world and enriches our lives in profound and meaningful ways. Adopting a constant attitude of gratitude can enhance our mental, emotional, and spiritual well-being, and help us navigate life's challenges with grace and resilience.

Benefits of Gratitude

1. **Improved Mental Health:** Gratitude reduces stress and anxiety, fostering a positive mindset. By recognizing and appreciating the positive aspects of our lives, we diminish negative thoughts and feelings of depression.

2. **Strengthened Relationships:** Expressing gratitude towards others strengthens bonds and improves communication. People who feel appreciated are more likely to respond with kindness and enhance interpersonal relationships.

3. **Increased Overall Well-Being:** Gratitude boosts our sense of satisfaction and happiness. It helps us appreciate what we have, rather than focusing on what we lack, and find joy in the small things in life.

How to Practice Constant Gratitude

1. **Keep a Gratitude Journal:** Each day, note a few things for

which you are grateful. This can include positive experiences, personal achievements, or interactions with others.

2. **Express Verbal Gratitude:** Make a habit of saying "thank you" more often. Thank people for their acts of kindness, big or small, and let them know you appreciate their presence and support.

3. **Reflect Daily:** Spend a few minutes each evening reflecting on the positive aspects of your day. This practice will help you end the day on a positive note and sleep better.

4. **Write Gratitude Letters:** Write thank-you letters to those who have had a positive impact on your life. Even if you don't send them, this exercise allows you to recognize and appreciate others' contributions.

Transformative Effects of Gratitude

1. **Change in Perspective:** Gratitude helps us see the world from a more positive angle. It encourages us to focus on what's going well rather than what isn't and develop an optimistic attitude.

2. **Enhanced Resilience:** When we cultivate gratitude, we are better equipped to handle challenges. By recognizing the positive aspects, even in difficult times, we find the strength

to persevere.

3. **Improved Quality of Life:** Constant gratitude enriches our lives significantly. It helps us savor each moment, develop deeper relationships, and live with a sense of peace and contentment.

Constant gratitude is a powerful practice that can transform our lives. By adopting a grateful attitude, we improve our mental health, strengthen our relationships, and increase our overall well-being. By integrating gratitude into our daily lives, we develop a more positive perspective, enhance our resilience, and enrich our quality of life. Gratitude reminds us that, even in challenging times, there is always something to appreciate and celebrate. Let's embrace constant gratitude and allow it to illuminate our path toward a more fulfilling and happier life.

The Benefits of Gratitude

1. **Improvement of Mental Health:** Gratitude reduces stress and anxiety, fostering a positive mindset. By recognizing and appreciating the positive aspects of our lives, we diminish negative thoughts and feelings of depression.

2. **Strengthening Relationships:** Expressing gratitude towards others strengthens bonds and improves communication. People who feel appreciated are more likely to respond with kindness and enhance interpersonal

relationships.

3. **Increased Overall Well-Being:** Gratitude boosts our sense of satisfaction and happiness. It helps us appreciate what we have, rather than focusing on what we lack, and find joy in the small things in life.

How to Practice Constant Gratitude

1. **Keep a Gratitude Journal:** Each day, note a few things for which you are grateful. This can include positive experiences, personal achievements, or interactions with others.

2. **Express Verbal Gratitude:** Make a habit of saying "thank you" more often. Thank people for their acts of kindness, big or small, and let them know you appreciate their presence and support.

3. **Reflect Daily:** Spend a few minutes each evening reflecting on the positive aspects of your day. This practice will help you end the day on a positive note and sleep better.

4. **Write Gratitude Letters:** Write thank-you letters to those who have had a positive impact on your life. Even if you don't send them, this exercise allows you to recognize and appreciate others' contributions.

Transformative Effects of Gratitude

1. **Change in Perspective:** Gratitude helps us see the world from a more positive angle. It encourages us to focus on what's going well rather than what isn't and to develop an optimistic attitude.

2. **Enhanced Resilience:** When we cultivate gratitude, we are better equipped to handle challenges. By recognizing the positive aspects, even in difficult times, we find the strength to persevere.

3. **Improved Quality of Life:** Constant gratitude enriches our lives significantly. It helps us savor each moment, develop deeper relationships, and live with a sense of peace and contentment.

Conclusion

Constant gratitude is a powerful practice that can transform our lives. By adopting a grateful attitude, we improve our mental health, strengthen our relationships, and increase our overall well-being. By integrating gratitude into our daily lives, we develop a more positive perspective, enhance our resilience, and enrich our quality of life. Gratitude reminds us that, even in challenging times, there is always something to appreciate and celebrate. Let us embrace constant gratitude and allow it to illuminate our path to a more fulfilling and happier life.

Keep A Vision Of Grandeur And Perfection

The vision we hold of ourselves and others has a profound impact on our lives and the relationships we build. Adopting a vision of grandeur and perfection, not only for ourselves but also for others, allows us to live with more confidence, inspiration, and human connection.

The Power of Personal Vision

1. **Improvement of Self-Esteem:** When we see ourselves in a positive light, we develop better self-esteem. This gives us the confidence needed to achieve our goals and overcome obstacles.

2. **Motivation and Perseverance:** A clear vision of our potential and grandeur motivates us to work hard and persevere, even in the face of challenges. It reminds us of what we are capable of achieving.

3. **Creation of Positive Realities:** By visualizing our perfection and success, we attract positive opportunities and create a reality aligned with this vision. Our thoughts influence our behavior, which in turn shapes our reality.

Seeing Grandeur and Perfection in Others

1. **Strengthening Relationships:** We strengthen our relationships by seeing potential and perfection in others. When people know we believe in them, they feel valued and inspired to give their best.

2. **Promoting Kindness:** Adopting this vision encourages us to be more compassionate and empathetic. We become more understanding and patient, creating a harmonious and positive environment.

3. **Stimulating Personal Growth:** When we see the best in others, we encourage them to grow and develop. Our positive vision can be a source of inspiration and motivation for those around us.

How to Cultivate a Vision of Grandeur and Perfection

1. **Affirmation Practice:** Use positive affirmations to reinforce your vision of grandeur and perfection. Repeat phrases like "I am capable and powerful" or "I see beauty and potential in myself and others."

2. **Daily Visualization:** Spend a few minutes each day visualizing your ideal life. Imagine yourself achieving your goals, living with confidence, and in harmony with those around you.

3. **Recognition of Successes:** Celebrate your successes, even the small ones. Recognizing your accomplishments helps maintain a positive view of yourself.

4. **Encouragement of Others:** Give sincere compliments and encourage those around you. Let them know you believe in their potential and ability to succeed.

Transformative Effects of This Vision

1. **Increased Confidence:** Maintaining a vision of grandeur and perfection increases your confidence in yourself and your abilities. This confidence is noticeable to others and enhances your charisma and influence.

2. **Creation of a Positive Environment:** A positive vision of oneself and others creates an environment of support and growth. People are more likely to cooperate and help each other when they feel valued.

3. **Attraction of Opportunities:** By constantly visualizing the best for yourself and others, you attract opportunities and positive experiences. Your optimistic attitude and energy draw favorable situations and kind people.

Keeping a vision of grandeur and perfection, both for yourself and for others, is a powerful practice that can transform your life and enrich your relationships. By cultivating this vision, you enhance your confidence, create positive environments, and attract favorable opportunities. The vision we hold guides our actions and shapes our reality. Let us choose to see grandeur and perfection in ourselves and others and live a life filled with success, happiness, and deep connection.

We Are, Of Nature, A Top Perfection

We are all endowed with immense potential and an intrinsic nature of perfection. This fundamental truth, often overshadowed by daily challenges and personal doubts, is key to unlocking our inner power and living a fulfilling and meaningful life.

Inherent Perfection Within Us

1. **Unlimited Potential:** Each of us possesses unique talents and extraordinary abilities. Our nature of top perfection lies in recognizing and harnessing these innate gifts.

2. **Divine Creation:** We are creations of a higher power, designed with care and precision. This belief strengthens our understanding of the perfection that resides within us.

3. **Reflection and Growth:** Our ability to reflect and learn from our experiences is evidence of our perfect nature. Each challenge we overcome and each lesson we learn brings us closer to realizing our full potential.

How to Embrace Our Perfection

1. Practice Self-Compassion: Be kind to yourself. Accept your imperfections as opportunities for growth rather than

flaws.

2. **Personal Development:** Engage in personal development practices such as meditation, reading, and ongoing education. These activities nourish our minds and strengthen our confidence in our innate perfection.

3. **Positive Affirmations:** Use affirmations to reprogram your mind and reinforce your belief in your perfection. Repeat phrases like "I am perfect just as I am" and "I am capable of achieving extraordinary things."

4. **Encourage Others:** Recognizing perfection in others also helps us see and celebrate our own. Be a champion of positivity and encouragement.

The Benefits of Recognizing Our Perfection

1. **Enhanced Self-Confidence:** Embracing our perfect nature develops unwavering self-confidence. This confidence allows us to take risks, seize opportunities, and overcome obstacles with resilience.

2. **Enriched Relationships:** When we perceive ourselves as perfect, we attract positive and fulfilling relationships. We interact with others authentically and kindly, creating deep and meaningful connections.

3. **Success and Abundance:** Recognizing our perfection opens

the door to abundance in all areas of our lives. We become magnets for opportunities, prosperity, and success.

Living in Awareness of Our Perfection

1. **Practice Gratitude:** Be grateful for your talents, successes, and the lessons learned. Gratitude strengthens our perception of perfection within us.

2. **Visualization:** Imagine yourself achieving your dreams and living your ideal life. Visualization is a powerful tool for aligning our minds with our perfect nature and attracting what we desire.

3. **Adopt a Balanced Lifestyle:** Take care of your physical, mental, and emotional well-being. A balanced lifestyle reinforces our connection to our nature of top perfection.

We are, of nature, atop perfection. By recognizing and embracing this truth, we unlock our potential and live a fulfilling and meaningful life. Practice self-compassion, engage in personal development, and use positive affirmations to reinforce your belief in your perfection. By living in awareness of our perfection, we enhance our self-confidence, enrich our relationships, and attract success and abundance. Always remember: you are a divine creation, perfect as you are, with the ability to achieve extraordinary things.

To Tell the Truth, We Are All ONE: The Great "I AM" in Action

In the grand tapestry of existence, a fundamental truth rises above all distinctions and separations: we are all ONE. We are part of a single universal consciousness, embodying the Great "I AM" in action.

The Unity of Existence

1. **Universal Interconnection:** Every living being, every thought, every action is intrinsically linked. We are individual expressions of a single universal consciousness, which means all separation is an illusion.

2. **The Great "I AM":** "I AM" represents the primordial creative force, the source of all existence. By recognizing ourselves as manifestations of this force, we understand our unity with the Whole.

3. **Love and Compassion:** Unconditional love is the glue that unites us. By embracing love and compassion, we realize our unified nature and transcend the barriers of ego.

Living Unity Daily

1. **Practice Meditation:** Meditation helps us connect with our inner essence and feel our unity with the universe. By

meditating regularly, we cultivate awareness of our unified nature.

2. **Affirmations of Unity:** Use affirmations like "I am a part of the Whole" and "I am an expression of the Great I AM" to strengthen your connection to unity.

3. **Acts of Kindness:** Every act of kindness is a recognition of our unity. By helping others, we help another facet of ourselves.

4. **Universal Gratitude:** Practice gratitude for all experiences and beings. Gratitude opens our hearts and reinforces our sense of unity.

The Benefits of Recognizing Our Unity

1. **Inner Peace:** By realizing our unity with the universe, we find profound inner peace. We understand that we are part of a greater plan and are always supported by the universal force.

2. **Harmony with Others:** Recognizing our unity fosters harmony in our relationships. We see others as extensions of ourselves, which reduces conflicts and enhances cooperation.

3. **Spiritual Awakening:** This realization is a key step toward spiritual awakening. We transcend the limitations of the ego

and live a more enlightened and conscious existence.

The Great "I AM" in Action

1. **Conscious Creation:** As manifestations of the Great "I AM," we have the power to co-create our reality. Use this power with intention and love to manifest positive experiences for yourself and others.

2. **Service to Others:** Serving others is a form of service to oneself. By offering help and support, we reinforce our unity and contribute to collective elevation.

3. **Inner Listening:** Learn to listen to your inner voice, the intuition that is the guidance of the Great "I AM." This guidance will always lead you to choices that support unity and harmony.

To tell the truth, we are all ONE. By recognizing our unity with the Great "I AM," we transcend the illusions of separation and live an existence enriched by peace, harmony, and universal love. Practice meditation, use affirmations of unity, and engage in acts of kindness and service. By living this truth daily, we contribute to the manifestation of a more unified and conscious world. Always remember: you are a unique expression of the Great "I AM," in constant action for the good of all.

Keep a Vision of Grandeur and Perfection Within You

The vision we hold of ourselves and others profoundly impacts our lives and the relationships we build. Adopting a vision of grandeur and perfection, not only for ourselves but also for others, allows us to live with greater confidence, inspiration, and human connection.

The Power of Personal Vision

1. **Improved Self-Esteem:** When we see ourselves in a positive light, we develop better self-esteem. This gives us the confidence needed to achieve our goals and overcome obstacles.

2. **Motivation and Perseverance:** A clear vision of our potential and grandeur motivates us to work hard and persevere, even in the face of challenges. It reminds us of what we are capable of achieving.

3. **Creation of Positive Realities:** By visualizing our perfection and success, we attract positive opportunities and create a reality aligned with this vision. Our thoughts influence our behavior, which in turn shapes our reality.

Seeing Grandeur and Perfection in Others

1. **Strengthening Relationships:** We strengthen our relationships by seeing potential and perfection in others.

When people know we believe in them, they feel valued and inspired to do their best.

2. **Promoting Kindness:** Adopting this vision encourages us to be more kind and empathetic. We become more understanding and patient, creating a harmonious and positive environment.

3. **Stimulating Personal Development:** When we see the best in others, we encourage them to grow and develop. Our positive vision can be a source of inspiration and motivation for those around us.

How to Cultivate a Vision of Grandeur and Perfection

1. **Affirmation Practice:** Use positive affirmations to reinforce your vision of grandeur and perfection. Repeat phrases like "I am capable and powerful" or "I see beauty and potential in myself and others."

2. **Daily Visualization:** Spend a few minutes each day visualizing your ideal life. Imagine yourself achieving your goals, living with confidence, and in harmony with those around you.

3. **Acknowledging Successes:** Celebrate your successes, even the smallest ones. Recognizing your accomplishments helps maintain a positive vision of yourself.

4. **Encouraging Others:** Give sincere compliments and encourage those around you. Let them know you believe in their potential and their ability to succeed.

The Transformative Effects of This Vision

1. **Increased Confidence:** Maintaining a vision of grandeur and perfection boosts your confidence in yourself and your abilities. This confidence is noticeable to others and enhances your charisma and influence.

2. **Creation of a Positive Environment:** A positive vision of yourself and others creates a supportive and growth-oriented environment. People are more inclined to cooperate and help each other when they feel valued.

3. **Attraction of Opportunities:** By constantly visualizing the best for yourself and others, you attract opportunities and positive experiences. Your optimistic attitude and energy draw favorable situations and benevolent people.

Keeping a vision of grandeur and perfection, both for yourself and others, is a powerful practice that can transform your life and enrich your relationships. By cultivating this vision, you enhance your confidence, create positive environments, and attract favorable opportunities. The vision we hold guides our actions and shapes our reality. Let us choose to see grandeur and perfection in ourselves and others, and live a life filled with success, happiness, and deep connection.

See Beyond: The Grandeur You Are Meant to Manifest

Within each human being lies immense potential, a grandeur waiting to be awakened and manifested. To realize this grandeur, it is crucial to see beyond apparent limitations and believe in the possibility of manifesting your highest aspirations.

The Vision of Grandeur

1. **Recognize Your Unlimited Potential:** Every individual possesses an infinite capacity to create, innovate, and transform their reality. Recognize your unlimited potential and believe in your power to manifest wonders.

2. **Creative Visualization:** Use the power of visualization to see beyond your current situation. Imagine with clarity and detail the grand life you wish to manifest. Feel this reality as if it were already present.

3. **Positive Affirmations:** Use affirmations to anchor your vision of grandeur. Tell yourself: "I am destined to manifest greatness," "I am capable of realizing my boldest dreams," and "I am creating an extraordinary life."

Steps to Manifest Your Grandeur

1. **Clarity of Intentions:** Be clear about what you wish to manifest. Define your intentions with precision and detail. A clear intention is the first step towards manifestation.

2. **Take Inspired Action:** A vision without action remains a dream. Commit to taking action, guided by your intuition and vision. Every small step you take brings you closer to your goal.

3. **Persistence and Resilience:** The path to grandeur may be filled with obstacles. Be persistent and resilient. Learn from each challenge and use it as an opportunity for growth and strengthening.

4. **Cultivate a Success Mindset:** Adopt a Success Mindset. Believe in your ability to overcome challenges and achieve your goals. Surround yourself with positive and inspiring people who support your vision.

The Benefits of Manifesting Your Grandeur

1. **Personal Fulfillment:** By manifesting your grandeur, you live a more fulfilling and satisfying life. You realize your potential and contribute significantly to the world.

2. **Inspiration for Others:** Your success and grandeur inspire those around you. By realizing your dreams, you show

others that it is possible for them too.

3. **Positive Impact:** By living your grandeur, you have a positive impact on your community and the world. You become a catalyst for change and improvement.

Seeing Beyond Limitations

1. **Overcome Fears:** Fear is often the greatest obstacle to manifesting greatness. Learn to overcome your fears by facing them and transforming them into courage.

2. **Expand Your Awareness:** Expand your awareness by exploring new ideas, continuously learning, and opening yourself to new experiences. The broader your awareness, the larger your vision of what is possible.

3. **Live in the Present Moment:** Learn to live fully in the present moment. The present is the only time you can act and create. By being fully present, you access an infinite source of creativity and power.

See beyond limitations and believe in the grandeur you are destined to manifest. By visualizing clearly, affirming positively, taking inspired action, and persisting through challenges, you can transform your boldest dreams into reality. Grandeur is within you, ready to be awakened. Manifest it with confidence, passion, and determination. You are capable of creating an extraordinary life, inspiring others, and having a positive impact on the world. Go beyond your expectations and embrace your unlimited potential.

See in your peers and surroundings the grandeur and top perfection.

See The Grandeur And Supreme Perfection In Your Peers And Surroundings

Every human being possesses a unique light, an extraordinary potential waiting to be recognized and honored. To create a harmonious and prosperous world, it is essential to see the grandeur and perfection in ourselves and in those around us.

The Vision of Grandeur and Perfection

1. **Recognize the Inner Light:** Every individual carries an inner light. Recognizing this light in yourself and in others is the first step toward a harmonious and enriching interaction.

2. **Cultivate Appreciation:** Take the time to appreciate the unique qualities and talents of those around you. This appreciation strengthens bonds and fosters a positive and constructive environment.

3. **Encourage Potential:** See the unlimited potential in each person. Encourage and support the aspirations and dreams of those close to you. Their success also reflects your support and belief in them.

Practices to See Grandeur and Perfection

1. **Active Listening:** Practice active listening with your loved ones. By being fully present and attentive to their words, you show that you value their perspective and existence.

2. **Positive Affirmations:** Use positive affirmations to reinforce the perception of grandeur in others. Tell them: "You are capable of achieving extraordinary things," "You have great wisdom within you," and "I believe in your infinite potential."

3. **Kind Actions:** Engage in kind and selfless actions. Small acts of kindness can have a tremendous impact on how others perceive themselves and how valued they feel.

Benefits of Seeing Grandeur in Others

1. **Strengthening Relationships:** By seeing and valuing the grandeur in others, you strengthen bonds of trust and love. Relationships become deeper and more meaningful.

2. **Creating a Positive Environment:** An environment where everyone is valued for their greatness and talents becomes a fertile ground for creativity, innovation, and collective prosperity.

3. **Collective Empowerment:** When everyone is recognized and encouraged in their grandeur, a dynamic of mutual

support and collaboration emerges. This leads to personal and collective growth.

Overcoming Obstacles

Letting Go of Judgments: Learn to let go of judgments and criticisms. See each person as a work in progress, with immense potential still to be unveiled.

Practicing Forgiveness: Forgiveness is essential to releasing emotional blocks that may cloud our vision of grandeur in others. Forgive yourself and others for past mistakes.

Cultivating Empathy: Empathy allows us to understand and feel what others are experiencing. This deep understanding enhances our ability to see and honor the grandeur in everyone.

Seeing the grandeur and perfection in your peers and surroundings not only transforms your perception of the world but also improves the quality of your relationships and environment. By cultivating a positive vision, encouraging each person's potential, and practicing appreciation and kindness, you contribute to creating a reality where grandeur and perfection are recognized and celebrated. Together, by seeing the best in others, we build a world of harmony, collaboration, and shared success. Embrace this vision and let the light of grandeur illuminate every interaction and relationship in your life.

Maintain A Vision Of Grandeur And Perfection

The vision we hold of ourselves and others has a profound impact on our lives and the relationships we build. Adopting a vision of grandeur and perfection, not only for ourselves but also for others, allows us to live with greater confidence, inspiration, and human connection.

The Power of Personal Vision

1. **Enhancing Self-Esteem:** When we view ourselves in a positive light, we develop a better self-esteem. This gives us the confidence needed to achieve our goals and overcome obstacles.

2. **Motivation and Perseverance:** A clear vision of our potential and grandeur motivates us to work hard and persevere, even in the face of challenges. It reminds us of what we are capable of achieving.

3. **Creating Positive Realities:** By visualizing our perfection and success, we attract positive opportunities and create a reality aligned with this vision. Our thoughts influence our behavior, which in turn shapes our reality.

Seeing Grandeur and Perfection in Others

1. **Strengthening Relationships:** By seeing potential and perfection in others, we strengthen our relationships. People feel valued and inspired to give their best when they know we believe in them.

2. **Promoting Kindness:** Adopting this vision encourages us to be more kind and empathetic. We become more understanding and patient, creating a harmonious and positive environment.

3. **Stimulating Personal Growth:** When we see the best in others, we encourage them to grow and develop. Our positive vision can be a source of inspiration and motivation for those around us.

How to Cultivate a Vision of Grandeur and Perfection

1. **Affirmation Practice:** Use positive affirmations to reinforce your vision of grandeur and perfection. Repeat phrases like "I am capable and powerful" or "I see beauty and potential in myself and others."

2. **Daily Visualization:** Take a few minutes each day to visualize your ideal life. Imagine yourself achieving your goals, living with confidence, and being in harmony with those around you.

3. **Recognition of Successes:** Celebrate your successes, even the small ones. Acknowledging your achievements helps maintain a positive vision of yourself.

4. **Encouraging Others:** Give sincere compliments and encouragement to those around you. Let them know you believe in their potential and ability to succeed.

Transformative Effects of This Vision

1. **Increased Confidence:** Maintaining a vision of grandeur and perfection increases your confidence in yourself and your abilities. This confidence is noticeable to others and enhances your charisma and influence.

2. **Creating a Positive Environment:** A positive vision of yourself and others creates a supportive and growth-oriented environment. People are more inclined to cooperate and help each other when they feel valued.

3. **Attracting Opportunities:** By constantly visualizing the best for yourself and others, you attract positive opportunities and experiences. Your optimistic attitude and energy draw favorable situations and kind people.

Maintaining a vision of grandeur and perfection, both for yourself and others, is a powerful practice that can transform your life and enrich your relationships. By cultivating this vision, you boost your confidence, create positive environments, and attract favorable opportunities. The vision we hold guides our actions and shapes our reality. Let us choose to see grandeur and perfection in ourselves and others, and live a life filled with success, happiness, and deep connection.

We Are Naturally of Supreme Perfection

We are all endowed with immense potential and an intrinsic nature of perfection. This fundamental truth, often overshadowed by daily challenges and personal doubts, is the key to unlocking our inner power and living a fulfilling and meaningful life.

The Inherent Perfection Within Us

1. **Unlimited Potential:** Each of us possesses unique talents and extraordinary abilities. Our nature of supreme perfection lies in recognizing and harnessing these innate gifts.

2. **Divine Creation:** We are creations of a higher force, designed with care and precision. This belief reinforces our understanding of the perfection that resides within us.

3. **Reflection and Growth:** The ability to reflect and learn from our experiences is evidence of our perfect nature. Every challenge overcome and every lesson learned brings us closer to realizing our full potential.

How to Embrace Our Perfection

1. **Practice Self-Compassion:** Be kind to yourself. Accept

your imperfections as opportunities for growth rather than flaws.

2. **Personal Development:** Engage in personal development practices such as meditation, reading, and continuous education. These activities nourish our minds and strengthen our confidence in our innate perfection.

3. **Positive Affirmations:** Use affirmations to reprogram your mind and reinforce your belief in your perfection. Repeat phrases like "I am perfect as I am" and "I am capable of achieving extraordinary things."

4. **Encourage Others:** Recognizing perfection in others also helps us see and celebrate our own. Be a champion of positivity and encouragement.

Benefits of Recognizing Our Perfection

1. **Enhanced Self-Confidence:** By embracing our perfect nature, we develop unwavering self-confidence. This confidence enables us to take risks, seize opportunities, and overcome obstacles with resilience.

2. **Enriched Relationships:** When we perceive ourselves as perfect, we attract positive and fulfilling relationships. We interact with others authentically and compassionately, creating deep and meaningful connections.

3. **Success and Abundance:** Recognizing our perfection opens the door to abundance in all aspects of our lives. We become magnets for opportunities, prosperity, and success.

Living in Awareness of Our Perfection

1. **Practice Gratitude:** Be thankful for your talents, successes, and the lessons learned. Gratitude reinforces our perception of perfection within us.

2. **Visualization:** Imagine yourself achieving your dreams and living your ideal life. Visualization is a powerful tool to align our mind with our perfect nature and attract what we desire.

3. **Adopt a Balanced Lifestyle:** Take care of your physical, mental, and emotional well-being. A balanced lifestyle strengthens our connection with our nature of supreme perfection.

We are of supreme perfection by nature. By recognizing and embracing this truth, we unlock our potential and live a fulfilling and meaningful life. Practice self-compassion, engage in personal development, and use positive affirmations to reinforce your belief in your perfection. By living in the awareness of our perfection, we enhance our confidence, enrich our relationships, and attract success and abundance. Remember always: you are a divine creation, perfect as you are, with the ability to achieve extraordinary things.

Truly, We Are All ONE: The Great "I AM" in Action

In the grand tapestry of existence, a fundamental truth rises above all distinctions and separations: we are all ONE. We are part of a single universal consciousness, embodying the Great "I AM" in action.

The Unity of Existence

1. **Universal Interconnection:** Every living being, every thought, every action is intrinsically linked. We are individual expressions of the same universal consciousness, meaning all separation is an illusion.

2. **The Great "I AM":** The "I AM" represents the primordial creative force, the source of all existence. By recognizing ourselves as manifestations of this force, we understand our unity with the Whole.

3. **Love and Compassion:** Unconditional love is the glue that binds us. By embracing love and compassion, we realize our unified nature and transcend the barriers of the ego.

Living Unity in Daily Life

1. **Meditation Practice:** Meditation helps us connect with our inner essence and feel our unity with the universe. By

meditating regularly, we cultivate an awareness of our unified nature.

2. **Affirmations of Unity:** Use affirmations like "I am part of the Whole" and "I am the expression of the Great I AM" to reinforce your connection to unity.

3. **Acts of Kindness:** Every act of kindness is a recognition of our unity. By helping others, we are helping another facet of ourselves.

4. **Universal Gratitude:** Practice gratitude for all experiences and beings. Gratitude opens our hearts and strengthens our sense of unity.

Benefits of Recognizing Our Unity

1. **Inner Peace:** By realizing our unity with the universe, we find a deep inner peace. We understand that we are part of a greater plan and are always supported by the universal force.

2. **Harmony with Others:** Recognizing our unity fosters harmony in our relationships. We see others as extensions of ourselves, reducing conflicts and enhancing cooperation.

3. **Spiritual Awakening:** This realization is a key step towards spiritual awakening. We transcend the limitations of the ego and live a more enlightened and conscious existence.

The Great "I AM" in Action

1. **Conscious Creation:** As manifestations of the Great "I AM," we have the power to co-create our reality. Use this power with intention and love to manifest positive experiences for yourself and others.

2. **Service to Others:** Serving others is a form of service to oneself. By providing help and support, we reinforce our unity and contribute to collective elevation.

3. **Inner Listening:** Learn to listen to your inner voice, the intuition that is the guidance of the Great "I AM." This guidance will always lead you towards choices that support unity and harmony.

Truly, we are all ONE. By recognizing our unity with the Great "I AM," we transcend the illusions of separation and live a life enriched by peace, harmony, and universal love. Practice meditation, use affirmations of unity, and engage in acts of kindness and service. By living this truth daily, we contribute to the manifestation of a more unified and conscious world. Remember always: you are a unique expression of the Great "I AM," in constant action for the good of all.

See another greatness that you are waiting to manifest.

See Beyond: The Greatness You Are Destined to Manifest

Within every human being resides immense potential, a greatness waiting to be awakened and manifested. To realize this greatness, it is crucial to see beyond apparent limitations and believe in the possibility of manifesting your highest aspirations.

The Vision of Greatness

1. **Recognize Your Unlimited Potential:** Each individual possesses an infinite capacity to create, innovate, and transform their reality. Acknowledge your unlimited potential and believe in your power to manifest wonders.

2. **Creative Visualization:** Use the power of visualization to see beyond your current situation. Imagine in clarity and detail the life of greatness you wish to manifest. Feel this reality as if it were already present.

3. **Positive Affirmations:** Use affirmations to anchor your vision of greatness. Tell yourself: "I am destined to manifest greatness," "I am capable of achieving my boldest dreams," and "I am creating an extraordinary life."

Steps to Manifest Your Greatness

1. **Clarity of Intentions:** Be clear about what you wish to manifest. Define your intentions with precision and detail. A clear intention is the first step toward manifestation.

2. **Take Inspired Action:** A vision without action remains a dream. Commit to taking action, guided by your intuition and vision. Each small step you take brings you closer to your goal.

3. **Persistence and Resilience:** The path to greatness may be filled with obstacles. Be persistent and resilient. Learn from each challenge and use it as an opportunity for growth and strengthening.

4. **Cultivate a Success Mindset:** Adopt a success mindset. Believe in your ability to overcome challenges and achieve your goals. Surround yourself with positive and inspiring people who support your vision.

Benefits of Manifesting Your Greatness

1. **Personal Fulfillment:** By manifesting your greatness, you live a more fulfilled and satisfying life. You realize your potential and contribute significantly to the world.

2. **Inspiration for Others:** Your success and greatness inspire those around you. By realizing your dreams, you show

others that it is possible for them too.

3. **Positive Impact:** By living your greatness, you make a positive impact on your community and the world. You become a catalyst for change and improvement.

See Beyond Limitations

1. **Overcome Fears:** Fear is often the greatest obstacle to manifesting greatness. Learn to overcome your fears by confronting them and transforming them into courage.

2. **Expand Your Awareness:** Expand your awareness by exploring new ideas, constantly learning, and opening yourself to new experiences. The more your awareness expands, the greater your vision of what is possible becomes.

3. **Live in the Present Moment:** Learn to live fully in the present moment. The present is the only time you can act and create. By being fully present, you access an infinite source of creativity and power.

See beyond limitations and believe in the greatness you are destined to manifest. By visualizing clearly, affirming positively, taking inspired action, and persisting through challenges, you can transform your boldest dreams into reality. Greatness is within you, ready to be awakened. Manifest it with confidence, passion, and determination. You are capable of creating an extraordinary life, inspiring others, and making a positive impact on the world. Go beyond your expectations and embrace your unlimited potential.

See the Greatness and Supreme Perfection in Your Peers and Surroundings

Every human being possesses a unique light, an extraordinary potential waiting to be recognized and honored. To create a harmonious and prosperous world, it is essential to see the greatness and perfection in ourselves and those around us.

The Vision of Greatness and Perfection

1. **Recognize the Inner Light:** Each individual carries an inner light. Recognizing this light in yourself and others is the first step towards harmonious and enriching interactions.

2. **Cultivate Appreciation:** Take the time to appreciate the unique qualities and talents of those around you. This appreciation strengthens bonds and fosters a positive and constructive environment.

3. **Encourage Potential:** See the unlimited potential in every person. Encourage and support the aspirations and dreams of your loved ones. Their success is also a reflection of your support and belief in them.

Practices for Seeing Greatness and Perfection

1. **Active Listening:** Practice active listening with your loved ones. By being fully present and attentive to their words, you show that you value their perspective and existence.

2. **Positive Affirmations:** Use positive affirmations to reinforce the perception of greatness in others. Tell them: "You are capable of achieving extraordinary things," "You have great wisdom within you," and "I believe in your infinite potential."

3. **Kind Acts:** Engage in kind and selfless actions. Small gestures of kindness can have a tremendous impact on how others perceive themselves and feel valued.

Benefits of Seeing Greatness in Others

1. **Strengthening Relationships:** By seeing and valuing greatness in others, you strengthen bonds of trust and love. Relationships become deeper and more meaningful.

2. **Creating a Positive Environment:** An environment where everyone is valued for their greatness and talents becomes a fertile ground for creativity, innovation, and collective prosperity.

3. **Collective Empowerment:** When everyone is recognized and encouraged in their greatness, a dynamic of mutual

support and collaboration is established. This leads to personal and collective growth.

Overcoming Obstacles

1. **Letting Go of Judgments:** Learn to let go of judgments and criticisms. See each person as a work in progress, with immense potentials yet to be revealed.

2. **Practice Forgiveness:** Forgiveness is essential for releasing emotional blockages that may cloud our vision of greatness in others. Forgive yourself and others for past mistakes.

3. **Cultivate Empathy:** Empathy allows us to understand and feel what others are experiencing. This deep understanding enhances our ability to see and honor the greatness in everyone.

Seeing greatness and perfection in your peers and surroundings transforms not only your perception of the world but also the quality of your relationships and environment. By cultivating a positive vision, encouraging everyone's potential, and practicing appreciation and kindness, you contribute to creating a reality where greatness and perfection are recognized and celebrated. Together, by seeing the best in others, we build a world of harmony, collaboration, and shared success. Embrace this vision and let the light of greatness illuminate every interaction and relationship in your life.

Recognize Your Authority Constantly

Recognizing and honoring your own authority is essential for living a fulfilling life aligned with your true potential. This recognition allows you to make informed decisions, act with confidence, and navigate life with unwavering clarity and determination. Here's how you can constantly recognize and affirm your authority.

The Importance of Recognizing Your Authority

1. **Self-Confidence:** Recognizing your inner authority strengthens your self-confidence. You feel capable of facing challenges and seizing opportunities with assurance.

2. **Clarity of Goals:** When you recognize your authority, your goals become clearer. You know what you want and how to achieve it.

3. **Autonomy and Independence:** By affirming your authority, you become more autonomous. You make your own decisions and take responsibility for your life.

How to Recognize Your Authority

1. **Daily Affirmations:** Use positive affirmations to remind yourself of your authority each day. Tell yourself: "I am the

master of my life," "I make wise and informed decisions," and "I have the power to create my reality."

2. **Inner Listening:** Take time to listen to your inner voice. Meditation and reflection can help you connect with your inner wisdom and strengthen your personal authority.

3. **Make Decisions:** Exercise your authority by making decisions, even small ones. Each decision made with confidence reinforces your sense of authority.

Practices to Affirm Your Authority

1. **Set Boundaries:** Learn to say no and set clear boundaries. This shows that you respect your time and energy.

2. **Develop Skills:** Invest in learning and developing skills that enhance your confidence and authority in various areas of your life.

3. **Express Your Opinions:** Don't be afraid to share your opinions and ideas. Your perspective is unique and valuable, and sharing it reinforces your authority.

Overcoming Obstacles

1. **Combat Self-Doubt:** Identify and challenge negative thoughts and doubts that may weaken your authority. Replace them with positive and affirming thoughts.

2. **Avoid Comparison:** Avoid comparing yourself to others. Everyone has their own path and talents. Focus on your strengths and accomplishments.

3. **Take Calculated Risks:** Don't be afraid to take risks. Mistakes and failures are learning opportunities that ultimately strengthen your authority.

Constantly recognizing your authority is a dynamic process that requires practice and self-awareness. By affirming your authority, you become the master of your life, capable of navigating with confidence and clarity. Cultivate this recognition through affirmations, conscious decisions, and deep inner listening. Respect your own boundaries, develop your skills, and express your opinions with assurance. By overcoming doubts and avoiding comparisons, you strengthen your authority and live a life aligned with your true potential. Remember, you are the master of your destiny, and the key to your fulfillment lies in recognizing and affirming your inner authority.

Recognize and Experience Your Glory

Every individual possesses a unique inner light, a personal glory that is waiting to be recognized and experienced. Embracing this glory means accepting your true potential and living a fulfilled and authentic life. Here's how you can recognize and experience your own glory.

The Importance of Recognizing Your Glory

1. **Personal Fulfillment:** Recognizing your own glory leads to deep personal fulfillment. You feel more aligned with your true essence and aspirations.

2. **Self-Confidence:** By recognizing your glory, you strengthen your self-confidence. You become more certain of your abilities and your worth.

3. **Positive Impact:** Your personal glory inspires others and has a positive impact on your environment. By living your truth, you encourage others to do the same.

How to Recognize Your Glory

1. **Introspection:** Take time to reflect on your talents, passions, and accomplishments. Acknowledge your successes and celebrate your unique qualities.

2. **Positive Affirmations:** Use affirmations to reinforce your recognition of your own glory. Repeat phrases like "I am unique and valuable," "My inner light shines brightly," and "I am worthy of all success and happiness."

3. **Recognize Your Talents:** Identify and value your talents and skills. These are aspects of your glory that set you apart from others.

Experiencing Your Glory

1. **Express Your True Self:** Be authentic in your actions and words. Let your true personality shine without fear or shame.

2. **Pursue Your Passions:** Engage in activities that excite and bring you joy. This allows you to fully live your glory.

3. **Help Others:** Use your light to assist and inspire others. By sharing your glory, you create a virtuous circle of positivity and growth.

Practices for Experiencing Your Glory

1. **Daily Gratitude:** Practice gratitude for everything you have and everything you are. Gratitude helps you recognize and appreciate your own glory.

2. **Visualization:** Visualize yourself living your best life, radiating glory. Visualization strengthens your belief in your

potential and attracts positive experiences.

3. **Journaling:** Keep a journal where you note your thoughts, achievements, and moments of gratitude. This helps you stay connected to your inner glory.

Overcoming Obstacles

1. **Combat Self-Sabotage:** Identify self-destructive thoughts and behaviors that prevent you from recognizing your glory. Replace them with positive affirmations and constructive actions.

2. **Avoid Negativity:** Surround yourself with people and situations that support and value your light. Avoid negative influences that try to diminish your shine.

3. **Take Risks:** Don't be afraid to step out of your comfort zone. The greatest experiences of glory often lie beyond your fears and limitations.

Recognizing and experiencing your own glory is a journey of self-discovery and affirmation. It is an ongoing process that requires self-awareness, introspection, and practice. By taking time to recognize your talents, using positive affirmations, and pursuing your passions, you can fully embrace and live your glory. By overcoming obstacles with determination and surrounding yourself with positivity, you strengthen your inner light. Remember, you are a unique and precious source of light. Live your glory with confidence and inspire the world around you.

Your Legacy is Unlimited: Here's the Proof

A simple calculation of the cost of the universe will give you an idea of your wealth.

Claim it now.

Understanding Your Share of Wealth According to the Distribution of the Universe

To divide 60 septillion by 8 billion, we first need to understand the values of these two numbers.

- One septillion is 10^{24}

- One billion is 10^9.

So,

- 60 septillion = 60×10^{24}

- 8 billion = 8×10^9

The division of these two numbers is then:

$$\frac{60 \times 10^{24}}{8 \times 10^9}$$

This simplifies to:

$$7.5 \times 10^{15}$$

So, 60 septillion divided by 8 billion is equal to 7.5 quadrillion (or 7.5×10^{15}).

How Much is 60 Septillion Divided by 10 Billion?

60 septillion divided by 10 billion equals 6 quadrillion, or 6,000,000,000,000,000. Here's how to break down this calculation:

Definitions:

1. **Septillion:** 1 septillion in American notation is 10^{24}.

2. **Billion:** 1 billion is 10^9.

Conversion to Numbers:

- **60 septillion** in numeric notation is 60×10^{24}.

- **10 billion** in numeric notation is 10×10^9.

Division:

To divide 60×10^{24} by 10×10^9:

$$\frac{60 \times 10^{24}}{10 \times 10^9} = \frac{60}{10} \times 10^{24-9} = 6 \times 10^{15}$$

Final Result:

Combining the coefficient and the power of 10: 6×10^{15}

In numeric notation, this reads as 6 quadrillion, or:

6,000,000,000,000,000

So ⊃ 60 septillion divided by 10 billion equals 6 quadrillion, or 6,000,000,000,000,000.

So,   Tell Me, Are You Not Rich?

If we consider the truth that human wisdom is more precious than gold and diamonds, aren't we immensely rich?

How can we explore this wisdom and put it at the service of humanity? It is by applying our talents and thoughts that spring from "The Thought of Eternity where God first thinks, and then Man reaps the fruits." Isn't this how our predecessors created everything around us?

The global population is projected to reach 8.5 billion by 2030, then increase to 9.7 billion by 2050 and 10.4 billion by 2100, according to United Nations demographic forecasts and statistics.

But the Son of God remains ONE, and grace lives in His Heart. All of us are the Only Son.

We are all heirs of creation as the Only Son. We are all equally rich.

As He is, so are we: ONE, The Power of Celestial and Eternal Unity.

Not bills but BILLIONS.

Edje BOUKA